How To Overcome Anxiety & Worry Through Mindfulness.

Deal with worry, stress, panic, fear & negative thinking.

Michelle Galler

Copyright © Michelle Galler Publishing

All rights reserved.
No part of this publication may be reproduced, distributed, or transmitted in any form or by any means, including photocopying, recording, or other electronic or mechanical methods, without the prior written permission of the publisher, except in the case of brief quotations embodied in critical reviews and certain other non-commercial uses permitted by copyright law.

Table of Contents

Conclusion: Starting Again

Beating Anxiety and Worry

"Yesterday is not ours to recover, but tomorrow is ours to win or lose."
Lyndon B. Johnson

Living life in a constant state of anxiety and worry is no fun at all. It curtails your enjoyment of even the simplest things as you fret about what might go wrong or how inadequate you feel. It doesn't take much to shift from being just about able to cope to being overwhelmed. By definition, the last straw that breaks the camel's back is a tiny, insignificant thing in itself, but a tiny thing too far when added to everything else weighing you down.
The good news is that there are strategies and approaches which can help. You can take back control. It won't happen overnight, but gradually you will find things are just that bit better. It's a journey towards rediscovering the joy in life, and an all-important first step on that journey is reading this book.

The 21st-century lifestyle is wonderful in many ways. We live longer than ever before, we have better education, healthcare, and housing than our predecessors. We can travel across the world in a matter of hours and be in touch with distant friends and family instantly through the magic of digital communications. There is a lot to be grateful for.

But our modern way of living is also incredibly stressful. Social media and the Internet can become an addiction, and the endless pressure to present your best self leading a dream life can lead to feelings of inadequacy and failure. We are bombarded 24/7 by information, far too much for us to consciously process. At work, the same digital devices that bring us entertainment and diversion make us constantly accessible, meaning we can never really switch off from the stream of *"urgent"* communications pinging, bleeping or flashing at us, demanding our attention.

An avalanche of media articles, TV shows, books, celebrity opinions, YouTube tutorials and guru blogs on every aspect of our personal lives from dating and relationships to child rearing and house interiors lead to us feeling like lesser beings if our homes aren't clutter-free and sparkling, our partners and children not perfect and loving and our bodies anything except lithe and youthful, clad in the latest designer must-haves. It can get utterly exhausting keeping up with the Millennials, no wonder we all want to crawl into a hole and hide sometimes!

Worry is an insidious and unhelpful emotion. It achieves nothing. Engaging in worry just makes you feel bad, which in turn makes you more likely to worry and less able to cope. It's a vicious circle that can be hard to escape. It takes a lot of determination to break the cycle of worry, but it is so worth breaking. Expending precious energy fretting about something that either may not happen or that you can do nothing about, really is a waste. Here's a little story to make the point.

Two friends, Kathy and Maria, invested their life savings in a company that looked like a good bet. For a while, things went well and then one day the company's shares nosedived. It looked like they would lose everything. They would find out at 4pm if they were bankrupt or not. Before everything happened, they had arranged to play a round of golf, and so they met in the golf course changing room. Kathy was singing as she changed into her golf clothes. Meanwhile, Maria was on her phone, worried sick. She looked at her friend.

"How can you even think about playing golf today? We could be penniless in a few hours," she said.

"Well," Kathy replied. *"We can't do anything until four. Yes, we may lose everything, or we may not. But it's out of our hands Maria. If I could do something, I would. But since I can't, I'm not going to waste energy thinking about it. I'm going to go out and whack a few balls! Coming?"*

"No, I think I'll stay here. Someone might have some news before four, I need to stay put and, well, you know…"

"OK, see you later," Kathy said and off she went. Maria didn't notice. She was trying to get online to check the latest figures.

Kathy spent the next few hours breathing in fresh air, getting some exercise and enjoying her hobby. She whacked some balls pretty hard too and released some tension that way!
Maria spent the time pacing up and down, checking her phone every minute or so and calling friends to discuss the dire situation. By five to four she had a headache and felt truly sick and exhausted. She slumped on the bench and was still sitting there when her friend returned rosy-cheeked from her round of golf…
What happened at four o'clock? Well, that isn't the point, is it?

Making the choice to take some action is a positive and decisive step in the right direction. If you decide that enough is enough and that you want to re-experience the bright side of life, then you are already half-way there. Once you have made the decision, then things become just that bit easier, as if the very act itself has the power to effect change.
If you read it all the way through, then this book will be your guide to combatting overwhelm, worry and anxiety. The first part looks at the background and the theory because it helps to understand what is going on in your mind when you get into this state. The second part is a series of practical techniques you can use immediately to improve things.

This isn't a promise to make everything in the garden of your life rosy. *Nothing* is easy and perfect all the time. We *all* have to deal with the thorns as well as the roses. But having the right attitude and strategies in place makes it possible to appreciate and focus on the beauty of the flowers rather than the ugliness of the weeds. Rooting out worry and cutting back anxiety slowly and systematically helps create a light, bright space for good things to grow.

So, with no further ado, let us don our metaphorical gardening gloves, roll up our sleeves and begin!

PART 1: BEATING ANXIETY & STRESS

In order to change, you first need to understand what you are dealing with.
This section of the book will give you a background and a foundation to build on.

The Defining Terms

"Every problem has in it the seeds of its own solution. If you don't have any problems, you don't get any seeds."
Norman Vincent Peale

It always helps to know what you're dealing with, because then you can decide on the best strategy. This part of the book is going to look at the problems associated with anxiety and stress and their causes.

The chances are that you feel as if you can't cope. Things may have slowly built up to such an extent that you now spend your whole time in a state of chronic anxiety. You may feel like it wouldn't take much for you to lose it altogether and that you are just keeping hold of things by the most fragile of threads.

If you feel like this, then you will be suffering from at least one of the following problems:
Overwhelm
Worry
Anxiety
Fear
Panic
Stress

Let's look at them in turn. Not to wallow, that's not good, but to put them under the microscope and understand how they are all inter-connected.

Overwhelm
The fact that we use the verb *"overwhelm"* to describe being swamped by a huge mass, usually water, gives you a big clue to its meaning when applied to someone's psychological state. The Cambridge English dictionary defines overwhelm as *"to cause*

someone to feel sudden, strong emotion."

The feeling of being overwhelmed can be a positive or a negative one. When you look at the starry sky above you on a clear night, it can be overwhelming, as can falling in love or being presented with an award. But the negative side of this emotional deluge is very unpleasant indeed. It is often used in a work context when the number of tasks you need to cram into one day threatens to swallow you up. Or you may feel helpless and powerless as you are bombarded from all sides by countless problems - *"the slings and arrows of outrageous fortune."* (Yes, even Shakespeare wrote about overwhelm!)

Feeling helpless is a common symptom of overwhelm, perhaps reawakening childhood memories of not being able to control your life. Very often we blame outside forces or circumstances rather than ourselves. You may say *"What next?"* as you open an unexpected tax bill, or *"why do these things always happen at the worst possible time?"* as the washing machine floods all over the cat.

Paralysis is a typical response to overwhelm. You may literally sit motionless, not knowing what to do next, or the paralysis may manifest as procrastination as you find yourself watching talking rabbit videos on YouTube instead of finishing your urgent report. Another reaction to overwhelm is to become super-busy, as if you can somehow overcome the feeling of helplessness by sheer willpower and hard effort. In this situation, super-busy usually does not equal efficient or careful. You may make stupid mistakes if working with your mind, or become very clumsy if doing physical work.

Worry and Anxiety
There is an interesting article in **Psychology Today by Guy Winch: 10 Crucial Differences Between Worry and Anxiety.** In this, he describes how there are different psychological states, and we actually experience them differently. *"We tend to experience worry in our heads and anxiety in our bodies,"* he writes, adding later: *"worry is verbally focused while anxiety includes ... mental*

imagery." Another interesting distinction is that *"worry often triggers problem-solving, but anxiety does not."* Winch's article goes on to explain that while worry can be short-term, controllable and often caused by realistic concerns, anxiety can be longer-term, cause serious emotional distress and can even *"jump from one focus to another."*

Fear and Panic

Fear is the feeling of being scared by a specific real or imagined danger. The focus is usually short term – the present and immediate future. If it spirals out of control fear can lead to panic. An example of a real fear would be getting hit by a train if your car breaks down on a level crossing. An example of an imagined fear would be that there is someone hiding under your bed as you lie there in the dark. Whether real or imagined, with fear, you want to escape from the situation, or avoid it in the first place.

Stress

"Don't stress me out!"
"I'm so stressed!"
"This is really causing me stress!"

We use the term *"stress"* a lot these days, probably without really understanding what it means.

Back in the days when we lived in caves, life was genuinely dangerous. There were myriad of scary things, from wild animals to hostile neighbors, ready to snuff us out in a heartbeat. When we detected a threat, our bodies flooded us with chemicals to enable us to fight or run. The three major stress hormones adrenaline, cortisol, and norepinephrine, were released, moving blood from non-crucial areas like the skin to crucial ones like the muscles, increasing arousal, heart rate, breathing rate and responses. All good news in a life-threatening situation. And once the danger was over the chemicals would dissipate and you could return to cooking mammoth meatballs or doing something creative with flint.

The world has moved on from the dinosaur age to the digital and now our *"threats"* are things like huge credit card bills or an impossible boss; not lions looking for lunch. But, sadly, in those thousands of intervening years, we poor humans have not changed that much. Our brains still flood us with stress hormones whenever a threat appears, even if it is not a genuinely life-threatening one. Because we can't work off the stress chemicals by running or fighting, they slosh around our bodies with nowhere to go. Ironically, what nature designed to save us is now hurting us. Adrenaline, cortisol, and norepinephrine cause all manner of symptoms, particularly if you are constantly in situations which *"stress you out"*.

Chronic stress is no good for you at all. Some of the main symptoms are:

- insomnia
- headaches
- digestive problems *(from nausea and diarrhea to constipation and bloating)*
- loss of appetite or overeating
- drinking alcohol more
- smoking more
- substance abuse
- low energy
- low sex drive
- weak immune system
- skin problems
- inability to concentrate
- inability to make decisions
- inability to finish things
- lack of interest in anything outside work
- irritability
- anger or suppressed anger

It is important to mention that not *all* stress is bad. Apart from helping in genuinely dangerous situations, some acute stress is beneficial and can help motivate you to achieve more, improve your performance and overcome obstacles. This good stress is called eustress, and it can feel exciting. A typical characteristic of eustress is that you have a lot of control over the outcome and feel you can cope. Afterwards, you may feel on a high, tingling with the thrill of success.

The Causes of Stress
There are many specific situations which you can immediately identify as understandable causes of negative stress. These include:
- death of a spouse or loved one
- divorce
- separation
- money problems
- conflict or problems with children, family or friends
- legal problems
- illness or injury (yourself or loved ones)
- unemployment or job insecurity
- being a victim of crime or abuse

Some causes of **positive** stress include:
- getting married
- changing jobs
- moving house
- having a baby
- retiring
- getting promoted
- winning or inheriting money

However, there are many other contributors to stress which you may not be aware of, but which chip away at you insidiously. Many of these are products of our 21st-century lifestyle and can include:
- information overload from email, internet, social media and other digital sources
- multi-tasking
- 24/7 news which is inevitably tragic or sensational and creates a feeling that the world is a dangerous and volatile place
- commuting and travel
- over scheduling
- perfectionism or unrealistic expectations *(perhaps created by*

celebrity culture, social media or mass media)
- fears and phobias

Real Life Case Study: Serena

Serena Harvey is 39 years old and lives in a small seaside town in the south of the UK. She has been married for two years and has just had a baby, Amelia. She used to work in advertising and her husband Mike is a woodcarver and artist. They live in a small two-bedroomed house a few miles from the town center, which has a tiny garden and is within walking distance of the shops and a park. She was always close to her parents, but her mother died three years ago, and her father isn't coping very well. Serena has been feeling increasingly stressed and anxious since Amelia was born. This is what she says:

"In two years, I have changed from being a career girl, owning my own flat and bringing home quite good money to being a wife and a mother. It has been a real shock to the system.

Don't get me wrong, I love Mike and Amelia to bits. I got married and had a baby relatively late so it's not like I haven't had time to enjoy myself and travel and feel free. Oh my God, just listen to me! Talking about feeling free as if I'm in prison. I know I should be counting my blessings. I have a roof over my head, a guy who loves me, a gorgeous little girl... I don't know what's the matter with me really. I just feel so stressed all the time, like I'm going to explode. I've seen the doctor and I know it's not post-natal depression or anything like that. My friend Natalie had post-natal depression and it's not something you mess around with. No, this is just feeling generally, oh I don't know, just anxious, on edge. Hard to know how to describe it really. I seem to have so many things to do every day, I don't know where the time goes. Sometimes I just feel completely overwhelmed."

From what we already know about major life events, it's not surprising that Serena is feeling stressed. She has had a baby, and her sleeping patterns and lifestyle have changed. You can imagine that Serena is tired and although it is three years since her mum died, she must be missing her, particularly as a grandmother to her little girl. Let's find out a bit more about what's going on:

"Mike is brilliant, he does as much as he can to help me, but he's just got a new commission for a series of sculptures and needs to focus on that. I envy him the fact he's working. I do miss my job. I mean it was crazy a lot of the time, but I enjoyed the drama and the ridiculous deadlines if I'm honest. And the sense of teamwork. I don't really see many people at the moment and a lot of my old friends are from work and our schedules are very different now."

"Our financial situation is pretty precarious as he's freelance. We've had to borrow on the credit cards to get stuff for the house and Amelia. I find that hard, I used to earn good money. I hate scrimping and watching every penny! We don't owe a lot, not like my friend Casey who owes more than 20 grand. But I hate owing money and what with that and the mortgage we don't have a lot of spare cash. My Mum left me a little bit, a few thousand, but that's all long gone."

Serena has financial worries to add to the mix. Not serious ones, her husband has a new commission and they bring in enough to pay the mortgage, but they can't spend without thinking.

In addition to the practical issues that are bound to be stressful for anyone – death of a parent, a new baby, some financial pressures – there are those individual stressors that are so subjective and powerful. Serena is used to being independent, relatively carefree and well-off, working in a fast paced and quite exciting environment. Now her husband is the breadwinner and she spends most of her day at home. Her language at the start, the talk of freedom and prisons, is quite revealing.

We will come back to Serena throughout the book as she is going to try some of the ideas and techniques and give her feedback. One important thing to emphasize, whatever situation you are in, is that you should not feel guilty or think there is anything wrong with you because you have these feelings. It means that you are human.

Chapter 1 Takeaways

In this chapter we have looked at:
- The main components of stress and anxiety
- How stress manifests itself and a list of common symptoms
- The main causes of stress, worry and overwhelm
- The Holmes-Rahe stress test
- A case study involving Serena, a stressed new mother and former career girl who is feeling guilty for missing her freedom and overwhelmed by her current life

Now that we have analyzed the components of stress, anxiety and worry we will tackle an area that is a constant cause of emotional overwhelm for a lot of us - relationships. They can be the cause of such joy, but also the cause of many of our problems. Let's try and understand why.

Chapter 2 - The Stress of Relationships

"Nobody can hurt me without my permission."
Mahatma Gandhi

There are many different kinds of relationship, and you probably bring different aspects of your personality and character to each one. How you behave with your work colleagues may be completely different to how you are with your cousins or your partner or even your dog! What won't change, however, are your fundamental values and your way of being.

Motivational speaker Jim Rohn says you are the average of the five people you spend the most time with. I would say that should be six people because the person you spend all the time with is…you.

The Most Important Relationship In Your Life

The most important relationship of all is the one you have with yourself. Like it or not, you are going to be in it for the long term! By definition, relationships involve more than one person, so how can you have a relationship with yourself? Well, you are made of many parts, a community of inter-connected members. You have a relationship with your body and a relationship with your mind.

It's interesting to consider who the *"you"* is in that last sentence. When you think to yourself: *"I feel stressed,"* who is the one noticing that you feel stressed? It would appear that there is an *"observer"* part of you that notices and comments on these things. In other words, because you can think about your thinking, it means you are not your thoughts and emotions; you are separate from them. This can be very liberating because you realize that there is an authentic *"you"* that can operate independently from all the chaos and crap surrounding you.

To develop a healthy and nourishing relationship with yourself, first of all, you need to become an observer of yourself, to notice what triggers certain behavior, what pushes your buttons. That doesn't mean you have to try and correct that behavior, simply to notice it. The more you do this, the more powerful your observer mind will become, and the weaker your unhelpful responses will become. If you practice observing what is going on in your mind on a regular basis, you will begin to develop new neural pathways which will strengthen over time.

Understanding the observer mind can be one of the most powerful things you can do to develop a good relationship with yourself. Other things to do are:

Practice self-care.
This concerns your physical body. Make sure you nourish yourself by eating well, drinking enough water, getting enough sleep and exercise.

Have fun and reward yourself.
Do things that make you feel good, smile or laugh out loud. If you want to play on the swings in the park – do it! Watch a funny movie or your favorite stand-up comedian on YouTube. Give yourself treats every day, like half an hour reading a great novel or eating a delicious bar of chocolate. You deserve it!

Learn to meditate.
It need only take a few minutes every day but can have an incredible impact on all aspects of your life.

Take time to dream.
What would you like to do? How would you like your future to look? Write or draw (or paste pictures of) your dream life. Then spend a few minutes each day just imagining…

Create.
It doesn't matter if it's baking a cake, painting a picture, carving a piece of wood, writing a poem or knitting. Try to make sure that by the end of every day, you have created something that didn't exist in the morning.

Be compassionate.
Be as kind and caring to yourself as you would to other people. If you have had a terrible day, then treat yourself gently, as you would with a good friend who is feeling down. Don't beat yourself up for not feeling lively, energetic and positive. You are a human being, experiencing all the highs and lows that entails.

Research ways to help with problems.
If you are suffering from anxiety and stress, then spend some time researching how best to deal with it. Reading this book is a good start!

Relationships With Partners

Your relationship with your partner can affect you profoundly, particularly if you spend a lot of time together.

Think about yourself and your partner like two circles. When you decide to create a long-term relationship, the circles will overlap because of the experiences and beliefs you share. What you want to ensure is that one circle does not eclipse the other, that your whole life is subsumed into that of your partner. There should always be a separate part of the circles which is your own private space. As the circles grow and expand, so should the shared part. But it should always be in proportion.

Change is an inevitable and necessary part of any exclusive relationship. Its management is critical to the success of that relationship. Maintain an interest in your partner, what they think, how they behave, what they enjoy, how they look. Don't take them for granted.

As someone grows and matures, they will naturally change. The person may also make an active effort to change some aspect of their life, for example quitting smoking or losing weight. But don't ever force anyone to change or think that you can wait it out, and once you have been together long enough you can impose your ideas and will on your partner. It is the basis of the old (and sexist) joke: *What three words about weddings sum up a bride's attitude towards her future husband? Aisle, altar, hymn!* The only person you can change in any relationship is yourself.

Anxiety can ruin an intimate relationship, making you doubt everything. Continually fretting about if your partner is faithful or really does love you will mean that you may constantly be seeking reassurance. Everyone needs some reassurance of course, but too much can turn into neediness, which is not an attractive trait.

Alternatively, anxiety may make you withdraw and not allow yourself to show any vulnerability. You may even provoke situations in order to *"prove"* to yourself that you were right all along and the relationship was doomed. You may even nip fledgling relationships in the bud before they have a chance to develop because you are worried about getting hurt if you give your heart away. It becomes a self-fulfilling prophecy.

A healthy relationship means both partners trust each other but can also be vulnerable with each other. You have to accept that you deserve to be loved and to be treated well. Your partner loves you, your quirky ways and your uniqueness. You don't have to be perfect, you just have to be yourself; that is good enough. And if by chance it isn't good enough, and you can see that they are trying to change you, then they don't deserve you.

It's so nice to be relaxed with your partner, even when you're in old clothes and your hair's a mess. Who wouldn't want to feel that comfortable with their special someone? But that doesn't mean you should stop making an effort. So, dress up sometimes like you did on the first date. Keep the spark alive! I know a couple who have been married for 16 years and they always dress up for dinner, even at home. They say it's a daily reminder not to take their relationship for granted. You don't have to go to that extreme, but a spontaneous gift, a loving touch or asking about their day *(and listening with attention to the answer)* go a long way to keeping an intimate relationship fresh. It also keeps anxiety at bay, because your attention is on making your partner feel loved and appreciated, not on how worried you feel.

Another thing you can do if you are feeling worried in your relationship is to practice the observer tactic I mentioned earlier. Watch yourself worry! Accept that everyone worries and that you are not a bad person for doing that. Then try something. Act as if you haven't got any worries at all. As if everything in your relationship is perfect. Even if you do it for only a limited time, like an hour, it is very powerful.

No relationship is perfect and if you're anxious, you won't want to address problems in case it causes everything to end. But sometimes you need to talk about things that are bothering you or they could, over time, develop into a serious issue. Little things are more damaging than big things because the big problems are often things that can be tackled together.

You need to look at how you handle issues that bother you. Always use the first person and say how something makes you feel, rather than dictating what the other person should or should not be doing. So, for instance, you say *"I feel quite upset when you don't answer my texts straight away,"* rather than *"you never answer my texts straight away. What's the matter with you? I always reply to you immediately!"*

Some issues can't be fixed. If the anxiety you are feeling is caused by a toxic or co-dependent relationship, if your partner abuses you mentally or physically or does anything other than support you and love you, then you need to acknowledge the damage it is doing to you and move on, even though it might be hard to accept.

Your Relationship With Your Kids

"We never know the love of a parent till we become parents ourselves."
Henry Ward Beecher

There is no bond on earth like that of parent and child and because of its unconditional nature, there is also no bond likely to cause you more anxiety, worry and pain. So how can you build a healthy relationship with your child?

One of the most important things you can do is to spend time with your kids. Be present. Actively listen to them and be there for them as a loving and stable anchor. That means not multi-tasking or interrupting their bedtime story or chat time to take a call from work. It also means regularly making sure you have free time for them, because quantity does matter, despite what they say about "quality time" being more important. Your kids need to know they are a priority in your life.

Trust is a crucial issue in a parent and child relationship, from when they are tiny to when they tower over you. Be a good example. Don't break promises or confidences. Trust that they are doing the best they can and believe them if they tell you something. That doesn't mean being gullible and letting them lie to you, but thinking the best of them and allowing them to make their own mistakes sometimes.

Children respond well to encouragement and praise, yet it is all too easy to yell and criticize. Be supportive and positive while still being realistic. Don't lead kids to believe they are always right or that they will never fail. Things go wrong, that's part of life. Making mistakes and not always getting what you have set out to achieve are good life lessons, because it's not what happens to you that's important but how you deal with it. Being realistic doesn't mean being negative. I have a friend, Jeanie, whose mother believes in always being *"realistic."* (Yes, the parent–child bond doesn't disappear just because you are an adult.) She regularly pours cold water on Jeanie's plans and ideas, often pointing out so many potential flaws that Jeanie gives up before she's begun.

If your relationship with your child is causing you anxiety, then take a step back and examine things objectively. When children are growing up they are trying to make sense of the world, testing boundaries and learning to understand their own emotions. They are childish! They may lie, or get angry and lash out at you, but it isn't usually personal. They don't really hate you and wish you were dead! Over-reaction is a part of being a child, particularly a moody, hormonal teen. Getting riled and shouting at them is not going to help matters. Keep as calm as you can, don't raise your voice, and remember *"this too shall pass."* You are the adult here; you are the one that should set an example of how to behave, rather than get drawn into a slanging match.

Often parents project their own hopes and dreams onto their kids, getting worried and frustrated when things don't work out or when they feel their child isn't putting in enough effort. Be careful you are not living your life through your child, for example, encouraging them to do something they are not interested in or good at because secretly you always wanted to do it but never could.

A very good piece of advice is to put yourself in your children's shoes, perhaps even trying to think back to when you were their age and how you felt. A five-year-old has very different concerns from a fifteen-year-old, so don't dismiss their feelings and tell them it doesn't matter. Maybe it does to them. That doesn't mean giving in and letting them have everything they want; it means acknowledging what they have said and then setting fair boundaries.

Apparently, having dinner together as a family is extremely beneficial, even if just one parent is present. Take time to eat with your kids, ideally at the table, rather than with food on your laps and the TV on.

It isn't rocket science to point out that kids and adults these days are absolutely glued to their cell phones or other devices. Social media is a big cause of anxiety too, so set a good example yourself. Beware

.mptation to use technology as a babysitter, particularly if your children are young. Introduce them to nature, to books and animals. Show them there is life away from the screen!

Children learn by example, so if you are feeling worried and anxious in your own life and show it, they will pick up on this and perhaps even copy it. Learning to manage your own fears and feelings is an excellent model for your kids. You can even get them to identify how they are feeling and teach them techniques to cope. For example, counting to ten before saying anything if they feel angry or taking a few deep breaths if they feel scared.

The Relationship With Family and Friends

"You can't choose your family, but thank goodness you can choose your friends," so the old saying goes. Your family has the power to bring great joy but also cause you to have a lot of self-doubt and anguish. Let's face it, no-one can push your buttons as effectively as someone who has known you since you were a little kid!

It is all too easy to get into serious fights with your siblings and parents or parents-in-law. In my own family, there are several past incidences of family members not speaking for months or even years. Life is too short for this. Every family problem affects your energy and tugs at your subconscious and it is worth reaching out and healing a rift. Unless you are actually suffering abuse and damage, physical or psychological, then mend fences, say sorry, even if something wasn't your fault, and build a relationship with them again. I remember my friend John telling me that his elderly mother and her brother hadn't spoken for years. Then his mother got seriously ill. *"I called up my uncle,"* he said. *"And I told him my mom was very ill. I asked if the worst happened, would he would come to my mother's funeral. He was very shocked and replied of course he would. I told him that if he would do that, then wouldn't it be better to visit while she was still alive and they could enjoy time together. He came over the following week."*

Family members and those grafted onto us by marriage or partnerships can be demanding, and you may feel the need to be always in control and perfect which will cause a lot of stress and anxiety. I am giving you express permission to leave the beautiful housework skills, magical cleaning ability and immaculate child-rearing to the gods and goddesses of this world. You are good enough. If the house isn't 100 percent tidy when the in-laws come round, so be it. No one is shooting at you. It is not a life or death situation. There will always be clean freaks who will run a metaphorical white-gloved finger over the tops of your doors to check for dust. Well, good for them. You may prefer to spend the polishing time playing with the kids or writing a poem or even just doing nothing. That is your choice. It is your life. You can't please everyone.

Friends are a gift and research has proved that the better your social life and the wider your circle of friends, the healthier and happier you are. Even those of us who adore being alone and would rather stay in with a good book than go to a party can enjoy spending time with people who make us feel loved and uplifted.
 It takes two to tango, and the same goes for friendship. It is a give and take process and even if you are feeling depressed and stressed, don't forget to call a friend on their birthday, send a note thanking someone who has been kind, or just remind someone that their friendship means a lot. It is also OK to ask for help if you are feeling down. This is something you might find hard to do if you are the one who usually cheers people up or is known for being the life and soul of the party. I know this from personal experience. You feel like your role is to be the comforter and not the one needing comforting. But you are entitled to ask for support if you need it and your friends may be delighted to switch roles for a change, even slightly relieved that you are not perfect and positive the whole time!

There is one caveat with friendships and that is to beware of the toxic kind. You know exactly what I mean. The person who makes you feel depressed every time you are with them. Who is negative and judgmental and critical. Who seems to think your role is to be their sounding board as they rant on about all the things that make them angry or depressed or upset or, or, or … There is only one thing to do with people like this and that is limit your contact with them! It can be hard to just cut a relationship off, so just make sure you are busy or make an excuse if they demand your time. No-one needs energy vampires.

Chapter 2 Take-Aways

All the types of relationship we have looked at have the possibility of causing you tremendous worry and stress or great happiness and fulfillment. Which one it ends up being is in your hands, because you are the one in charge of your emotions and how you respond. In this chapter you have learned:

- The most significant and long-lasting relationship is the one you have with yourself. So be true to yourself. Don't fake anything.

- You need to limit or end toxic or co-dependent relationships.

- In relationships, particularly intimate ones, you must not be afraid of being yourself.

- Neediness can spoil things. You are worth loving.

- In all relationships, be assertive and explain what you need.

- That children need attention, time and encouragement. Be a good example.

- How relationships are a two-way process.

- The power of laughter and doing things that bring you joy.

- How anything worthwhile takes work and time.

In the next chapter we'll look at how you can get to know yourself better and make plans to change the way you react to worry and stress. Let's take a deep breath and dive in!

Chapter 3 - Creating Your Future

"They always say time changes things, but you actually have to change them yourself."
Andy Warhol

Changing isn't as difficult as you think. The hardest thing is actually making the decision to change. We can produce endless excuses, we can procrastinate like champions, we can convince ourselves that *"it's better the devil you know,"* in order to avoid taking that all-important step!

You purchased this book because you are not happy with how your life is at the moment. You have recognized that you are allowing anxiety and worry to play too big a role in your life. That, in itself, is significant. You don't have to criticize yourself or beat yourself up about it. Wanting things to be better than they are now is a very positive acknowledgment. No-one is perfect, we all have flaws and problems to deal with. Stage one is to own up to the issue and you have done that.

The next stage is to admit that things can't go on as they are. We all deserve to live the most fulfilled life possible and make the most of all the amazing opportunities that surround us. We need to have enough inner strength to be able to deal with the lows as well as the highs, because life isn't always all sunshine and rainbows. If you are governed by fear and worry, then all your energy will go towards feeding those negative emotions. You will be constantly tossed around on a gray sea of negativity. It has to stop. In its place, you need equilibrium and a calm center.

The good news is that you have all the tools at your disposal to help you change. There are many things you can do to improve your situation. They don't cost any money and they aren't that hard to follow. All you need do is resolve to try them, to give them a chance to work. That's fair enough, isn't it? It's amazing how empowered you will feel once you start practicing a few of the techniques that will be outlined in this book.

Your brain will begin to make changes very fast as it learns new modes of operating. You will build up new neural networks. Your subconscious will get the message that you are someone who responds to situations in a positive and proactive way and this will get reinforced the more you do it.

Aristotle famously said, *"We are what we repeatedly do."* Things we repeatedly do are, of course, habits. In some ways, our whole lives are governed by habits, some we are conscious of, some not. Habits which benefit us are positive and helpful, however we usually have a load of habits that are not making our lives better or more meaningful, quite the reverse. American author and philosopher Henry James wrote in his essay Habit in 1887: *"The great thing, then, in all education, is to make our nervous system our ally instead of our enemy. It is to fund and capitalize our acquisitions, and live at ease upon the interest of the fund. For this we must make automatic and habitual, as early as possible, as many useful actions as we can, and guard against the growing into ways that are likely to be disadvantageous to us, as we should guard against the plague."*

An important thing to do is to examine your habits, keep those that are beneficial, ditch those that are not and replace them with new, good habits.

Research shows that it takes between 21 days and 66 days to develop a new habit to the stage where it becomes automatic. The length of time depends on how complex or demanding the new habit is. If, for example, you want to drink an extra glass of water every day, you could probably make that an automatic part of your routine in three weeks, because it isn't that challenging a task. If you want to regularly monitor your thoughts and stop yourself in the act of negative self-talk, it will take longer than that. But as with anything, persistence pays off. Setting a time frame is a good idea. If you are the type of person who likes lists, plans and written targets then you will feel very comforted and motivated by having a strategy in place, even if you only take baby steps.

Talking of baby steps, there is a book called **Mini Habits** by *Stephen*

Guise, based on the idea that taking tiny actions consistently every day can achieve great results. The author himself achieved peak physical fitness in two years by starting with just one push-up a day. Sometimes the thought of change can be so overwhelming and such a mountain to climb that you end up doing nothing. Getting into the habit of doing one *"small silly thing"* regularly every day can have a huge impact. It's like the old saying, *"How do you eat an elephant? One bite at a time."*

Dealing With Your Issues

The Greek philosopher Socrates once said that *"the unexamined life is not worth living."* What did he mean by that? After all, the language is quite extreme! I think he was pointing out that as human beings we need to take time to reflect on our own lives, identify our personal values, habits, strengths and weaknesses. Taking some time to think constructively about your life and identify the areas needing improvement is a very useful exercise. Yet surprisingly few people do it.

What are the main things you want to change? As this book is about removing anxiety and worry from your life, then we will focus on those areas, rather than looking at your whole life. It's all too easy to get sucked down rabbit holes and get distracted from the main task. However, you can apply these techniques to all aspects of your life, once you have dealt with anxiety.

It is quite normal to worry about everyday issues; work, money, health, your family and so on. But if those worries become excessive and stop you functioning normally, then it is time to tackle them. When you find yourself anxious about every single thing, when you imagine murder, natural disaster or fatal accident if your partner is late or your child doesn't call, rather than the more likely scenario of forgetfulness or a switched-off cell phone, then maybe you need to do something about it.

It's a good idea to buy a notebook *(yes, the paper kind that you use with a pen!)* and use it to chart your issues and progress. Let's begin by looking at a list of things that might trigger your anxiety. Think about each one and over the next few days note down any thoughts and feelings you have and what you have observed.

Note down the time of day, the time of month, the time of year. There's lots of food for thought here. For example: Is there a particular time of day when you feel jittery? Could it be linked to certain drinks, food or being hungry? Or to darkness or light? The syndrome Seasonal Affective Disorder *(SAD)* is a well-known one, linking depression and dark moods to short winter days. Does a full moon have any effect on you? If you are of child-bearing age, how does your monthly period affect your mood?

Sleep: Are you getting enough? Do you dream or have nightmares? Maybe an anxiety dream triggers a waking mood of worry? Can you link different moods with your sleep patterns? Is your bedroom a calm haven and your bed a welcoming and cozy place? You may not take Feng Shui seriously, but they have a point regarding not having electronic devices in the bedroom, having a tidy space, not sleeping under beams and not having loads of stored items under your bed.

Health: You may not know it, but some physical health conditions produce anxiety as one of the symptoms, for example, an over-active thyroid, heart disease or high blood pressure. If you have any worries about your health, **have a check-up**. Do any foods, drinks or medicines trigger feelings of anxiety? Personally, Italian espresso coffee makes my nerves jangle and my heart race as well as making me feel extremely anxious, so I rarely drink it.

People and Their Habits: Are there people in your life who make you feel anxious or worried after an encounter with them? I have a friend who is very kind-hearted and generous, but has such a negative world view and is so critical of everyone and everything that I feel depressed every time we meet up! Do any family members trigger feelings of anxiety because of your past experience with them? Perhaps when you were a child, your grandmother was very superstitious and if she saw one sole magpie, would tell you terrible things would happen. These things go deeper than you imagine, and your unexplained and sudden feeling of gloom yesterday could be linked to a single black and white bird you didn't even think you had noticed consciously! The same goes for beliefs about money, work and family. If your parents were very concerned whenever a bill arrived then you could be producing the same response whenever a bill for you arrives, even if it is expected and you have enough money to pay it.

Your Environment: Is your living space clean and tidy? Spending a lot of time in an untidy, cramped or dirty environment can have a significant negative effect on you. If the corner of your living room is piled with bills and other unfiled paperwork, or you have stacks of laundry waiting to be ironed, boxes to unpack and so on, it can easily make you anxious and depressed. Every time you see this mess it will have an impact, even if you are not conscious of it. Do you have access to outside or to nature? Greenery, even pot plants, is a mood booster as well as helping you concentrate. Fresh air and sunshine not only boost Vitamin D but also make you feel better. Is your environment full of "sound and fury" or quiet and relaxing? Noise pollution can be as damaging as the physical kind. What can you see around you and how does it make you feel? Certain colors are more calming than others. Possessions and artwork can affect you because of the actual subject matter or the person you associate it with. If your bitchy mother-in-law gave you a painting then you will probably think of her every time you look at it, even if it is beautiful in itself!

Your Habits: As mentioned before, we are shaped by our habits, both good and bad. Do you do things mindlessly which may be having a negative impact? Maybe you always switch on the news at 7 o'clock because – well, you just do – and so your day starts with a depressing flood of nasty, anxiety-producing stories which don't personally affect you, but are presented as if they do. Do you add additional and unnecessary steps into a simple process, causing unneeded complication? It was only when I explained to my pet sitter that my dogs had a cup each of dogfood in the mornings, then a certain type of chew, then two small splashes of milk (not one, not three, but two) but that in the evening they had a cup of dogfood, a different chew and just one splash of milk otherwise they got upset, that I realized perhaps I was making a rod for my own back!

Major Life Events: Remember the stress test we did before? If you have had any of those things happen to you over the last 12 months then you are going to feel some degree of anxiety and stress on a daily basis. Inevitably, certain things, for example anniversaries, places or even music, will trigger feelings related to the event. It's quite normal, all you need do is note down when it happens in your notebook.

Sorting Through Your Anxiety Triggers

Once you have made notes over a few days, you can start to look at your personal stress and anxiety triggers and see if you notice any patterns. What you discover may surprise you. Just by doing this you have already taken an enormous step in reducing the stress in your life, because being aware of the problem is half the battle.

The next thing is to select one area to work on. Don't try to tackle it all at once even if you feel motivated to do so, because inevitably you will lose impetus and feel overwhelmed. Remember the elephant – one bite at a time!

This book will help, you can read it through first and then select the techniques you feel best suit the area you are working on. The exercises have been designed to be used in any sequence, so just pick something you feel drawn to. Not everything will be appropriate or suit your learning style. That's why it's important to have some idea about the kind of activities you enjoy doing and what kind of learner you are. Some people are highly visual, so enjoy any activities which involve images, drawing or creating mind pictures. Others work best with words and sounds, so will feel more drawn to exercises involving writing or music. Some of you are more kinesthetic, preferring to move around and try things out. *(You're the kind who will be playing around with the pieces of the wardrobe to see how they might fit together rather than reading the instruction manual!)* The point is, know yourself and your learning style and then use techniques to match. This includes your preferred time of day to practice. Be kind to yourself. Give yourself the best possible chance of success.

Talking of success, it's important to visualize a positive outcome after having eliminated one area of stress from your life. How would things change if worry about this problem was no longer an issue for you? What could you do? How would you feel? Imagine yourself happy and relaxed, ready to take the next step. If it helps you, then hand over your doubts and questions to a higher power – God, the Universe, it doesn't matter what you call this source of energy and love, just believe that your efforts are being guided and that you are not in this alone. It is achievable. You can do it.

Real Life Case Study: Remember Serena from Chapter 1? She's a 39-year-old former career girl and new mother who is feeling constantly stressed, but also feels guilty about feeling that way because she has a lovely little girl, a husband who adores her and a roof over her head. Serena decided to keep a small notebook handy and note down her stress and worry triggers and anything else she was feeling.

Time of day, time of month, time of year. As she did this in November, Serena noted that the dark mornings and evenings made her feel depressed and edgy. She remembered this was always the case and not just because of the new baby and the house move. Maybe she had Seasonal Affective Disorder? She circled "SAD" in her notebook as something to research later.

Sleep: This section made Serena laugh. What new mother gets enough sleep? She had always felt moody if she didn't get at least six hours, even when she was *"young, free and single"* so it wasn't surprising that night after night of interrupted sleep would affect her. She reasoned that it wouldn't last forever, in fact she had already noticed that Amelia was sleeping for a little longer each night.

Health: Serena had complete medical exams throughout her pregnancy and so knew that she was in general good health and had no underlying medical issues. She knew that pasta and wheat products made her lethargic and bloated and that dark chocolate could keep her awake, but in general she didn't really associate her anxiety with food or health.

People and Their Habits: Serena's father always used to say she had *"champagne tastes and a beer income"* and her mother, who had died so very recently, got incredibly anxious whenever bills arrived, particularly if she thought she had forgotten to pay them. Towards the end, she used to say she was terrified of going to prison is she was late paying a bill. This made Serena think. When she was working in advertising, she spent freely, without thinking. She made good money and basically had no-one to spend it on but herself. She always paid her bills on time and, quite unusually she thought, she only had one credit card, which she always paid in full every month. During the few days she was writing in her notebook several envelopes arrived, which her husband left unopened with the comment *"know what those are, don't need to see them!"* Serena noticed how upset and edgy this made her feel. She always opened the bills and faced the worst, it really annoyed her that Mike had a more relaxed attitude to money. She hated the fact they were living on one salary and had to struggle for money. Detested the fact they had bought stuff for Amelia and the new house with credit cards. She realized that she was behaving as anxiously as her mother used to, even worrying about losing their home or going to court because they couldn't pay their debts. *"Hmm,"* she said to herself as she underlined 'money' over and over again in her notebook. This was causing her a lot more stress than she had realized.

Your Environment: Serena's house was small, but she thought it was as tidy as it could be, considering the baby and all the things both she and Mike had brought with them from their previous single lives. It also had a little garden and lots of plants, as she and Mike loved being outside and nature. There was a lovely park nearby that she often went to with Amelia. She thought she probably got a good dose of fresh air and Vitamin D every day, so a big tick for that part! She looked around the room. Actually, there was quite a lot of stuff, including some ornaments and small items of furniture from her dear Mom's house which she wanted to have around to remind her of her childhood. She sat chewing her pen. Was she also hoping to hang onto her Mom's memory by keeping her stuff? She looked at one wall of the living room, which was almost a carbon copy of a wall in her Mom's place. She thought about how kind Mike had been when she started putting up Mom's clock and shelves and pictures. The house was really too small. It did make her feel kind of anxious when she saw all that stuff.

Your Habits: Serena thought long and hard about this part. She knew she wasn't suffering from OCD or any other type of compulsive disorder. Despite Mom's keepsakes, she wasn't a hoarder and she didn't need to do things a certain number of times or wash her hands a lot. She wasn't afraid of outdoors and although she enjoyed having her meals at set times – breakfast at 7, coffee at 11, lunch at 1, afternoon tea at 4 and dinner at 7 – she didn't think that was unusual. Was it? She remembered how she felt if this meal routine was disrupted. Very anxious. Hmmm. Amelia had certainly thrown her meals schedule out the window. Why was she so attached to this eating routine anyway? She circled this in her notebook, as something to do more thinking and research about as she felt it was one of her triggers.

Major Life Events: Serena made quick notes about the obvious major things that had happened to her within two years: a wedding, a death, leaving her job, a birth, a house move. *"It's surprising I can even get through the day in one piece with all that lot going on!"* she smiled to herself.
After reading through her notes, Serena decided she was going to focus on reducing her anxiety over money as that was something that she was clearly getting very affected by. She reasoned that she couldn't really do anything about the life events, and that the other things could be tackled one by one. As a very visual person who also loved words and who was at her best in the early morning, she decided to start with exercises that matched her preferred learning style and to try them when she awoke at 6. We'll see how she gets on as we go through the book.

Chapter 3 Takeaways

In this chapter we have looked at:
- How taking the decision to change because things cannot go on as they are is an important step.

- The importance and power of habits and how long it takes to establish a new habit.

- Examining your life and identifying your stress and worry triggers

- How Serena tackled the stress triggers exercise and what she discovered about the sources of her own worries.

Now that you have looked at your own stress triggers and identified an area that you want to work on, you are ready for Part Two of the book; **Strategies for Success**. There you'll begin putting some of the ideas into practice. Ready?

PART 2: STRATEGIES FOR SUCCESS

This part of the book uses the knowledge from Part One as a foundation for different techniques to tackle worry and anxiety.

Chapter 4 - Creating Space and Making Changes

"Most of us are inclined to keep too many old and useless things in our houses and in our minds as well…"
Emily Tolman

It's hard to overestimate the importance of space, both inside and outside of us. We need a clear and clean environment if we are to thrive. Fill that inner or outer space with clutter, with *"stuff"*, and we will soon find it hard to move and hard to breathe.

Very often someone's physical space will reflect their mental one. In a kind of vicious circle, your worry or anxiety will feed off that pile of unpaid bills or unopened mail in the corner of your living room. Stress will build as you subconsciously note all the things in your home that need to be repaired or thrown away. You may have a junk drawer, or a junk room, where you toss all the things you don't know how to deal with. Overwhelmed by the enormity of the task of clearing everything, you find it hard even to tidy one cupboard, which just makes you feel more anxious and annoyed with yourself.

Despite all the 21st-century services devoted to organizing and clutter clearing and the myriad gurus who want to save us from ourselves, clutter isn't a new problem. The Emily Tolman quote which opens this chapter is from a housekeeping book written in 1907. But the need to hold on to things whether we need them or not certainly dates back far earlier than that. Our prehistoric ancestors probably found it just as hard to part with their stuff. There's probably a huge junk room under Stonehenge filled with broken axes, granny's past-their-best loom weights and old mammoth tooth necklaces with bits missing!

The reasons that we keep things are as numerous as the boxes in a hoarder's basement. The most common ones are feelings of;

scarcity (*"I won't throw that away in case it comes in handy one day"*)

indecisiveness *("I'm not sure I want to throw that away in case I regret it, so I'll just keep it")*

guilt *("My mom gave me that and even though I've never liked it, I'd better keep it in case she finds out and gets upset")*

sentimental attachment *("I can't throw away my kids' school books, even though they have told me to!")* or

emotional reassurance (*"I feel comforted and reassured when I am surrounded by my collection of tiny teapots and Princess Di memorabilia".)*

Clutter in your mind is characterized by jumbled thoughts and incessant negative self-talk. You can't differentiate between the trivial and the important, everything is given equal weight. You think about the past, fret about the future, regret decisions you have taken and worry about ones you haven't taken yet.

This mental clutter comes from our own thoughts, but it also comes from external sources. As the Digital Age has come into its own, we have become subjected to an endless stream of data. A study by the University of California indicates that every day people are inundated with 34 gigabytes of information, equivalent to about 105,000 words, plus pictures, videos and games. The average American spends over 10 hours a day looking at a screen of some form or other, (*smartphone, laptop, tv, radio, DVD, video games*), with our children close behind at six and a half hours and growing. Although we don't absorb all this information, in the average American's life, it is there, everywhere, all the time. Small wonder our minds feel like dusty attics stuffed full of cobweb-covered boxes of thoughts and ideas.

When thinking about clutter, people often forget about digital clutter. Emails, crammed calendars, old files, downloaded games and films, e-books you have never read … just because it isn't physically taking up space in your house does not mean it isn't harmful.
You may think that clutter is a fact of life and that it may not be that bad. After all, how can possessions, ideas or information in our

physical, mental or virtual space have an effect, unless we allow them to?

Physical clutter can be a health danger, the dust and dander it collects are not good for people with allergies or asthma, for example. In extreme cases, it can lead to accidents *(some people have literally died after being crushed by their possessions)* and can be a fire hazard. Clutter can cause us to feel guilty or embarrassed that we haven't dealt with it, or frustrated as we fail to locate our keys or the latest bill from the insurance company under a pile of stuff. It makes us feel psychologically hemmed in and overwhelmed, constantly sending our minds the message that there is work to do and we haven't done it. It is also a constant sensory distraction, we see it, we may smell it, we touch it as we move it around or out of the way. It should be obvious by now, clutter is not a relaxing thing to deal with.

A 2016 study by Catherine Roster and colleagues at the University of New Mexico showed that many people identify very strongly with their homes and tend to be unhappy when they feel their home environment is overcrowded. The authors conclude that *"clutter …can threaten to physically and psychologically entrap a person in dysfunctional home environments which contribute to personal distress and feelings of displacement and alienation."*

Clearing Clutter from Your Physical Space

Nineteenth-century English textile designer, poet and novelist William Morris said, *"Have nothing in your houses that you do not know to be useful or believe to be beautiful."* It is an excellent starting point when deciding to tackle clutter. Just think about his words for a moment and see if they make sense to you and if you feel you can divide all your possessions into these two categories.

Japanese tidying guru and New York Times bestselling author Marie Kondo has her own twist on this. She asks you to touch or hold each item and ask yourself *"does it bring me joy?"* It's such a simple little technique which may not work for household essentials like hammers and pliers (for those, revert to William Morris and his *"useful"* definition), but can certainly have effects far beyond simply tidying.

I have used Marie Kondo's method and can recommend it. If you have been avoiding clearing clutter then this makes it quite fun. First of all, forget tidying anything away. You can tidy once you have finished clearing clutter. Kondo recommends tackling clutter according to the type of object rather than room by room or drawer by drawer. In her opinion, clearing clutter is not something you should be returning to over and over again. Once should be enough and then you monitor everything else on an ongoing basis. She also recommends not beginning the process (and it is a process that could take weeks or even months) with any possessions that you have an emotional attachment to. Her thinking is that as you become better at selecting items that bring you joy and getting rid of the rest, then you will become better prepared to tackle the things that are harder to throw away because of your strong emotional ties to them, such as gifts or inherited items.

 If you are to deal with your clothes, then Kondo advises taking all your clothes from all over the house and putting them into a big pile on the floor. Then you go through them one by one and apply the *"joy"* question. If this seems like too big a task then you can subdivide a category, so "clothes" could be broken down into "underwear" or "socks," for example.
Having done this myself, I can assure you that it is pretty easy to feel the joy. You know as soon as you touch something if you love it or not. It is also very easy to know if something is useful, even if it doesn't bring you joy. The textbook you need for college, the vacuum cleaner, the bottle of bathroom cleaner – they don't make you happy but perhaps the results of using them might.

What about the items that you hold up and then hesitate about. According to Kondo, something brings you joy or it doesn't, you know immediately if it does and any uncertainty means it doesn't. Marie Kondo may be small in stature and softly spoken, but she is quite a tyrant when it comes to being ruthless about clutter. She recommends immediately discarding the item or giving it away. That can be harder than you think. Your mind will play all kinds of tricks, inventing any number of reasons why you shouldn't do this. Maybe you will regret getting rid of it. Maybe you will learn to love it. Maybe you haven't given it a proper chance, you weren't really concentrating when you looked at it the first time. Maybe you should keep it because your partner, kids, friends love it. And so the list of excuses goes on. Because that is what they are – excuses.

If you are struggling with some possessions, then give yourself a bit of a break and create a *"not sure"* pile. Live with the pile for a few days, then redo the exercise. Hold each item again and ask if it brings you joy. (Or is useful). You might find it easier to get rid of things the second time around. If not, then rinse and repeat. What you are left with, apart from the useful things, is a reduced number of possessions which all please you or make you smile. That is such a great feeling.

What I like about this method is that it is so personal. You will hear many clutter-clearing gurus tell you, for example, to get rid of all the books you have read and probably won't read again as they are just dust gatherers and you should have spaces on your bookshelves. I have always loved books, not just because of the knowledge they contain but also as beautiful objects in their own right. To me it seems nuts to throw away books just because I have read them. They may be clutter to some people, but not to me. Using the Kondo method, I can simply go through and see which books give me joy or are useful. That is a much better approach than throwing all those volumes out and having empty bookshelves. To me, empty bookshelves look sad.

Everyone has a level of clutter they feel is acceptable and this is not something to feel guilty about. Some people are very minimalist by nature, love clear surfaces and nothing on show. Others are maximalist and are happier surrounded by more things. It's an entirely subjective and personal choice and is absolutely fine, as long as all the items around you make you feel happy or have some function. That is the bottom line really.

Having your environment as you like it, clean and filled with the possessions you love will have an immensely positive effect on your mind and body, so choose a tiny, achievable category and get started now.

Clearing Clutter from Your Mental Space

Clearing physical clutter is straightforward even if it is sometimes not that easy. The process is obvious, you identify something, remove it and then there is more space.
When you clear mental clutter, you are not removing objects, you are removing invisible things. You can't pick thoughts or fears up and you can't see when they are gone, so you need a different strategy to deal with them.

Think back to a time when you felt very calm, centered and relaxed. It may have been during a vacation or a happy period in your life. You may have been aware at the time that you were focusing on the moment and not worrying about the past or the future. That is the feeling that you want to have on a regular basis, when your mind is not stuffed full of anxiety and negative thoughts. That is why it is worth clearing the clutter from your mind.
You can't separate your mind from your body and one of the best things you can do to create a clearer and less cluttered mind is to take care of your health. That means eating well, getting plenty of sleep and taking regular exercise. Remember your triggers in the last chapter? You may have noted that you feel more anxious if you are hungry, so eat! If white wine makes you feel like crap and gives you a fuzzy head the next day, then stop drinking it. In other words, take care of the obvious physical stuff before you tackle the inner space.

Deep Breathing, Yawning and Stretching.
Mark Waldman, who teaches the Neuroleadership program at Loyola Maymount University is the author of 14 books and is one of the world's leading authorities on spirituality and the brain. Among the many brain exercises he advocates is this very simple 30-second one, to be done about three times an hour or whenever you have an

important decision to make or are feeling stressed. Simply yawn widely and mindfully two or three times and then take a deep breath and do some slow stretches, like you do when you wake up in the morning. Yawning with intent has been shown to lower stress and anxiety and releases neurochemicals and increases blood flow to the brain. Waldman says, *"It's hard to find another activity that so positively impacts so many functions of your brain."*

Repeat a Positive Values Word.
Another of Waldman's simple but highly effective techniques is to identify your own most important value and then use it to calm yourself and switch moods. To do this relax, breathe deeply and close your eyes. Ask yourself *"What is my deepest and most fundamental value?"* and then accept the first answer you get. As often as you can, particularly if you feel anxious or are being bombarded with negative thoughts, repeat this value word. (For example, it might be "love" or "peace" or "creativity".) To be effective you need to use positive words five to seven times more often than negative thoughts and worries, so every time you feel a depressing thought coming on, just repeat your word over and over. The brain can't handle two contradictory thoughts at the same time and the positive will override the negative.

Write Things Down.
If things are getting overwhelming, it can be very helpful to write them down. Seeing things on paper gets them out of your head and also gets them back in proportion. Look at your list of problems and worries and then think of your values word again. Watch as those problems shrink in size.

Make a Plan and Prioritize.
I love a plan! If I am feeling deluged by too many tasks, then I divide a piece of paper into four sections labeled: urgent and important, urgent and not important, important not urgent, not urgent and not important. Then I put all the tasks I have to do that day into the appropriate section, breaking them down into achievable chunks. I start with urgent and important, then move to urgent and not important and so on. It helps me feel back in control.

Deep Work and Focus.
As a counter movement to the 21st-century disease known as multi-tasking, there is *deep work*. Although the concept of deep work has been around for a long time, the term was coined by author and computer science professor Cal Newport in his book of the same name. Deep work means working with focus and no distractions on one cognitively demanding task. People who practice deep work switch off email, cell phones, and any other distractions and then concentrate intensely, for between one and four hours.

Build in Time to Daydream and Play.
It may seem contradictory, but Newport and Waldman both advocate taking time out to daydream and switch off. Our brain can achieve great leaps of creativity and problem-solving in this so-called down time. History is crammed full of stories of people who have made their greatest discoveries or had their best ideas while relaxing or daydreaming. Einstein used numerous thought experiments to play with theories of physics, the most famous being when he imagined he was traveling on a beam of light, an imaginary game which eventually led to his famous General Theory of Relativity. In a world where busyness is valued over playtime and inactivity, make a stand for doing nothing!

Do a Digital Detox.
Did you know that there are some luxury hotels now offering digital detox weekends? They will take away your smartphone and laptop and then suggest itineraries which will help soften the blow of being deprived of these precious objects. They are even reintroducing board games! You don't need to go to a hotel or pay hundreds of dollars to do this, but you do need a bit of willpower to ditch your devices. Set a time limit and then watch with wonder as the world unfolds in all its glory and proves to you that you can be there without needing the selfie to prove it.

Create a Sanctuary.
Find a quiet spot and relax. Close your eyes and then create in your imagination a special sanctuary, a place you can feel safe. It can look be anywhere you wish – up a mountain, in a forest, by the ocean, in a penthouse, even in the sky - and be furnished in whatever way

makes you happy. You can return to this place whenever you want, as often as you want, and you will always feel calm, safe and protected.

Meditate.
There are numerous articles, courses, and YouTube videos online about meditation, so Google them and find one that suits you, or see if there are any meditation classes near you. One thing is certain; it is very good for your brain and your health, it calms you down and relieves stress long term. A very simple meditation involves relaxing completely by stretching then relaxing each part of your body in turn, then focusing on breathing in for six seconds, hold for six seconds and breathe out for six seconds. The idea is to focus on your breathing and to be aware of the thoughts moving through your mind, but not dwell on them. Just doing this for a short time every day will reap benefits.

Listen to Music.
Not just any music. Baroque music like Bach or Handel, with 50 to 80 beats per minute, can help you access the calming alpha brainwave state. There are also soundtracks which use binaural beats available online. These are best listened to using headphones as they rely on each ear hearing a slightly different frequency, this creates the effect in the brain of a third sound, which is the difference between the two frequencies being played into the right and left ears. The brain will then produce brainwaves at the same rate of Hertz as the new sound. Binaural beats can help the brain enter different states, including deep relaxation.

Get Creative.
Make a cake, paint a picture, sculpt a fairy from modeling clay. It doesn't matter what you do, but try to get hands-on creative every day. Apart from the satisfaction of producing something that didn't exist until you brought it into being, getting creative is also very good at destressing and relaxing you. My husband relaxes by cooking amazing meals after work, and I relax by eating them!

Chapter 4 Takeaways

In this chapter we have looked at:

- How your physical and mental space reflect each other.

- The importance of having clear, clean space both in your environment and in your mind.

- What clutter is and why it doesn't help you.

- Techniques to help declutter your physical space, including choosing to keep only things that are useful or bring you joy.

- Techniques to help declutter your mental space.

We have discussed a lot about how the mind loves to dwell on the past or the future, causing you to feel guilt, regret or anxiety and worry. One of the most powerful ways to tackle this is to master the art of mindfulness. That's what we are going to look at in the next chapter.

Chapter 5 Mindfulness – This Changes Everything

"Begin at once to live, and count each separate day as a separate life."
Seneca

Mindfulness seems to be the buzzword of the moment, but what exactly does it mean? Basically, to practice mindfulness, you put all your attention and awareness on what is happening right now, in the present moment. You pay attention to your thoughts, feelings, physical sensations and sensory input and to what is going on in the world around you.
You may think that you are mindful all the time, but very few of us are. Unless you are using a chainsaw, walking a tightrope or doing other activities requiring concentration and attention, the chances are your mind is distracted, teeming with internal chatter and thoughts of the past or the future.

In the East, mindfulness has been an important part of many spiritual practices, particularly Buddhism and Yoga, for thousands of years. In the West, *Jon Kabat-Zinn* has been credited with bringing it mainstream relatively recently. He founded the Center for Mindfulness at the University of Massachusetts Medical School and created an eight-week Mindfulness-Based Stress Reduction Program and writes and lectures extensively on the subject. Other figures who have had an impact on western thinking include Eckhart Tolle who wrote the best-seller The Power of Now.

If you think about it, all we have is the present moment. We experience this in different, subjective ways. It can seem endless if we are bored or under stress, all too short if we are enjoying ourselves or saying goodbye to someone we love. We can miss the present moment completely if we are performing routine activities that result in us *"switching off"*. I'm sure all of us have experienced the sensation of arriving at work and not having the faintest idea how we got there. Obviously, we handled a car, navigated traffic and arrived safely. But the journey itself? A total blank.

We can miss things happening in the present moment for reasons other than routine or habit. In one of the best-known psychology experiments of recent years, conducted at Harvard University in 1999, people were asked to watch a video of a basketball match. There were two teams, one in white shirts and the other in black. The observers were asked to count how many passes the team in white shirts made. After the short video was played, the observers were asked if they had noticed anything unusual. This is because, during the game, a gorilla (*well, a guy in a gorilla suit*) had walked across the screen, faced the camera, thumped his chest and left, spending a total of nine seconds in view. The jaw-dropping result was that half the observers just didn't notice it! They were so distracted by their counting task that they just blanked the big hairy beastie. It's quite astonishing that we miss so much and equally surprising that half the time we have no idea that we have missed anything at all.

Why is mindfulness important? Does it really matter that much if we miss stuff, or allow our minds to dance back into the past or spin into the future? The answer seems to be yes, it does matter. Mindfulness has been shown scientifically to increase feelings of well-being, reduce anxiety and worry and improve sleep. It has a positive effect on both physical and mental health and people who consciously practice mindfulness are generally more content and able to form better relationships with others.

Simple Techniques for Everyday Mindfulness

Because of the nature of our lives these days, we need constant reminders to stay mindful. Here are a few suggestions for incorporating mindfulness into your day.

Mindfulness Bell
There are free apps and websites which will sound a beautiful ringing bell tone at regular intervals. This is great if you are doing computer work. Set the bell to ring two or three times an hour and when you hear it, even mid-sentence, take a break, yawn, stretch and focus for a minute or two on your body and how you are feeling.

You can get up and walk around the room, or jog on the spot for 30 seconds, or give yourself a quick but gentle head massage. It brings you back into the present moment and also refreshes your body and brain. Try http://awakeningbell.org/ for an online version.

Highlight Your Senses
This is quite an interesting exercise to try and you can also use it if you can't sleep. Sit or lie comfortably and take a deep breath. For five minutes focus on only one of your senses. Let's use sight as an example. Pay acute attention to everything that you can see, notice detail, light, shade and pattern in things you normally don't give much thought to. Look at places you don't usually notice, like the corner of the ceiling. Let your eyes follow a shape all the way around. Notice different shades of color and how the colors change according to the light on them or their position in the room. Bring all your focus to that one sense of sight, ignore the other four senses as much as possible. When the five minutes is up, then do the same for each of the other senses in turn. This is incredibly relaxing and may become one of your favorites!

Walk
Fresh air is very good for you and so is exercise, so going for a daily walk is already a great idea. Walking in nature is the ideal, but you can walk regularly wherever you are. Instead of walking along immersed in your thoughts and missing everything around you, walk with attention. Feel the ground under your feet and the way the muscles in your body are working. Feel the wind on your face. Smell the earthy goodness of the woods or the damp of the grass. Touch the plants as you pass, feeling the difference between ferny fronds and rough bark. If there are wild strawberries around, then taste a few, or taste the fresh air and the sweetness of the rain. Look around you. Really look. As poet William Henry Davies said, *"What is this life if, full of care, we have no time to stand and stare."*

Bathe with Intent
Your daily bath or shower is a great time to practice mindfulness. Rather than just racing through this routine, pay attention to what you are doing, seeing and feeling, smelling and touching. Imagine that you are washing away negativity and stress and starting the day

fresh.

Eat with Attention

We are all guilty of bolting our food down, especially if we are in a rush. In my case, I get quite annoyed with my body if I get hungry and just want to eat anything quickly to remove the hunger pangs and get on with what I was doing. *(Yes, I know, foodies are always horrified when I confess this!)* But eating with mindfulness can not only de-stress you, it can also help you lose weight. Whatever you are preparing and eating, give it your full attention. If you are making something, then imagine you are adding a generous portion of love to each ingredient. Watch how the flour floats down like a white cloud and how the golden yolks of the eggs change color as they mix with the sugar. I won't get too poetic about this, you get the message I'm sure.

When eating, savor every mouthful, chew and really taste what you are eating. There are five different tastes: salty, bitter, sour, sweet and umami (Japanese for "yummy") which is a kind of meaty taste usually produced by glutamates. (Who knew?) See if you can recognize them as you are eating. That's quite a fun one to try with kids too!

Scan Your Body

It's all too easy to ignore what your body is telling you when you are rushing around like a whirling dervish. Take a couple of minutes to mentally scan your body from your head to your toes and just note how each bit of you is feeling. You are not only looking for aches, pains and tension, but also feelings of relaxation or comfort too. If you find any sore points, then see if you can rub or massage them to feel better. Your body will appreciate it.

Do Nothing

We are so conditioned to fill every waking hour with busyness that we have forgotten how important it is to just do nothing, even if it for just a minute or two. Sit and look out of the window, watch the birds flying and the leaves of the trees moving, if you are lucky enough to have that view. If not, watch the traffic below or the little insect on your windowsill. If you have any thoughts, then just accept them and let them go.

Ditch the Tech

Spend as long as you can without your smartphone, laptop or tablet, whether that is five minutes or five hours. Whenever we have a break the temptation for most of us is to check our phones or surf the net. Don't. Do one of the activities I've just listed instead.

A Key Principle To Change

Mindfulness is not only being aware of what is around us and what we are feeling physically and mentally. It also involves appreciating the good things in life and being grateful for the smallest blessings.

Most of us express gratitude when we get a gift, or someone does something nice for us. This may even extend to writing a thank you note or email or sending a card to show your appreciation. However, practicing gratitude in a mindful way means being thankful every day, or several times a day, without having a reason. It makes you actively look around you and value all the things in your life that you normally take for granted, like sunshine and rain, having a roof over your head, not living in a war zone, having clean water to drink and being able to read and write.

These may seem very simple, even banal, things to focus on, but positive psychology research has shown that grateful people sleep better and are healthier both physically and psychologically. Gratitude is a great stress buster too. In fact, a 2006 study in Behavior Research and Therapy conducted with Vietnam War veterans showed a lower rate of PTSD (*Post Traumatic Stress Disorder*) amongst those with higher levels of gratitude. Grateful people have increased feelings of well-being, peace and self-esteem and are less aggressive. In other words, they feel happier! They are also less likely to be materialistic and more likely to be social too. Oh, and in case you need more evidence, grateful people live longer!

A Positive Change

As a way to move your focus away from the things bothering you and onto more positive aspects of your life, try writing down things you are thankful for. A list, a journal, a letter to yourself. And here's the proof.

The Emmons Lab, under the direction of Dr. Robert Emmons,

Professor of Psychology at the UC Davis, California is engaged in *"a long-term research project designed to research and disseminate a large body of scientific data on the nature of gratitude, its causes, and its potential consequences for human health and well-being."* They have published reams of research material to back up the positive effects of gratitude and are currently focusing on the development of gratitude in children.

Their researchers discovered that people keeping weekly *"gratitude journals"* took more regular exercise and generally felt more optimistic about what might be coming up in the next week than those who didn't. They were also more likely to have moved forward on the achievement of personal goals.

Keeping a gratitude journal or simply listing the things you are grateful for on a regular basis is simple, free and has proven scientific effects. It's kind of a no-brainer really. Try to get into the habit of listing the things you are grateful for every night before you go to sleep or as soon as you wake up in the morning. Why not give it a try now? Think of ten things that you are grateful for in your life.

Being grateful is even more effective if you write it down, so take a few minutes every day to write down what you are lucky to have in your life. Don't just repeat the same things every day either. Being innovative with your list makes you focus creatively on all the good there is in your life.

A Helping Hand On Your Journey

If you are an animal lover, then keeping a pet is an excellent way to de-stress. A South African study in 2003 conducted by the late Dr. Johannes Odendaal found that the simple act of petting a dog releases feel-good hormones like endorphins, oxytocin and norepinephrine. Dr. Odendaal concluded the same would happen if petting a cat. Endorphins are your body's natural opiates and relieve stress or pain.

Animals are taken into hospitals, old folks' homes and hospices for the same reason. Their presence helps comfort and relax patients, bringing a sense of calm and pleasure. Just being near a dog or cat lowers blood pressure. They don't just have to be dogs and cats. Other species, including alpacas and llamas, are trained as pet therapy animals too and the effect they have is incredibly positive and uplifting.

If you are stressed because you have too many things to take care of and too many people depending on you, then looking after a pet is probably not going to alleviate your problems. But that doesn't mean you have to forego the benefits of being with animals. A 2014 study from Washington State University showed that working with horses significantly reduced the stress hormone cortisol in children. The students who participated in the research spent 90 minutes a week with horses, either riding, grooming or interacting with them. There was also a control group who did not have anything to do with the program. After three months, the cortisol level of the kids working with horses had dramatically reduced. Even if you are no longer an adolescent, this will work at any age. You don't have to own or look after a horse yourself, you can take riding lessons or even spend time with them and get a similar effect.

Why does spending time with animals help alleviate stress? Animals keep you in the moment. They take the focus off you and make you feel less lonely and more loved. They give you immediate feedback in terms of wanting to play or enjoying a cuddle. They live in the moment themselves and don't hide their feelings, if an animal is happy or upset, you know it. If you are responsible for an animal, as opposed to just visiting one, then you have to make the effort to get up every day, feed it exercise it and take care of it. It can give some depressed people a sense of purpose and a reason to keep going.

Some animals are particularly sensitive to people in a depressed state or with certain issues like ADHD or autism and will actively seek them out and attempt to bond. People with autism enjoy the physical communication they can have with therapy animals, particularly horses, and these interactions provide a bridge to more normal communication with people too.

Many well-known animal "whisperers", like Mexican dog expert Cesar Millan and Austrian horse specialist Klaus Hempfling, have added human communication and self-confidence coaching to their array of skills because they understand that so many lessons from the natural world can also be successfully applied to people.

You can learn therapeutic massage techniques, like *The Tellington Touch*, to use on your pet. This gentle and relaxing method is extremely simple to learn and it will benefit both of you. Your pet will love being massaged and you will love the destressing effect it has on you as your cortisol levels reduce and your happy-hormone levels zoom upwards!

De-Stressing

Pets can really help you to de-tress. Make time every day to consciously connect with your pet. Spend a few minutes petting, grooming or massaging your companion animal.
Play with your pet! You will forget about your woes for a little while and have some fun and exercise.

Watch kittens, puppies or other young animals. If you don't have access to the real thing then watch some videos on YouTube. (Yes, this kind of digital entertainment I will allow!) There is a story that King Charles 1 of England asked for kittens to be brought to his cell so he could watch them playing the night before his execution to take his mind off things, so if it worked for him…

If you don't have a pet, then volunteer at the local shelter, or do some dog walking or pet fostering so you can still get regular contact with animals without the responsibility of owning one.

Sign your pet up to be a therapy animal. If they pass the test, (not all animals are suitable) then going with them to visit the elderly or ill will bring out the best in both of you.

If you don't know how, then learn to ride. If you do know how then start riding again. You don't have to bring yourself up to Olympic dressage standard, just enough for a gentle hack through the countryside will do.

An important thing to mention here is that animals take you out of yourself. They stop you from getting too inward looking and self-focused. Not everyone is an animal person, but if you are and you don't have a pet at the moment, then do consider how much good it will do you. In case you are worried about who will look after it when you want a holiday or have to work away, don't forget there are several websites connecting pet lovers who want to travel with pet owners who want someone to look after their home and animals. It's usually a mutually beneficial arrangement that is free of charge. So now you don't have any excuses!

Chapter 5 Takeaways

In this chapter we have looked at:

- What mindfulness is and its origins

- Why mindfulness is important in tacking stress and anxiety

- Techniques to incorporate mindfulness into your everyday life

- The power of gratitude

- How animals can help with mindfulness

Earlier we discussed how watching animals play, and actually playing with them, is great fun and very beneficial. Fun is such an important part of tacking stress and anxiety that I thought it deserved a chapter all of its own. Get ready to laugh!

Chapter 6 – The Power of "Fun"

"The human race has only one really effective weapon, and that is laughter."
Mark Twain

When you are stressed, worried or anxious, probably the last thing on your mind is having a good laugh and yet that is one of the best things you could do. Now, I'm not claiming that chuckling away at your favorite sitcom is going to cure all your physical or mental issues, but scientific proof of the benefits of laughter is unequivocal and growing all the time.

Laughter, smiling and generally feeling happy all help suppress the stress hormones like cortisol and adrenaline and release the good ones like endorphins and serotonin. Being aware of the power of laughter is important, because it can lead you to deliberately incorporate lighter moments into your day. You can't plan for funny things to happen to you, but you can plan to watch a funny sitcom for an hour every evening to make yourself feel better.

Did you know that the physical act of smiling has some very positive physiological effects on your brain and that of other people? Apart from being contagious, because it stimulates one of the unconscious automatic response areas in the brain, smiling also makes other people view you in a more positive light. A 2011 study by a team at the Face Research Laboratory at the University of Aberdeen proved that men and women found images of people more attractive when they were smiling and making eye contact. We know from personal experience that interacting with a smiling person is a lot more pleasant than someone who looks upset or just plain angry. It's very hard to keep your face twisted into a frown or scowl if someone is openly smiling at you, because it seems nature has programmed us to reflect a smile back so both parties enjoy that surge of positive neurotransmitters. The important thing to remember is that you don't need to feel happy to smile, but smiling will tend to make you feel happier. It might sound odd to smile when you feel miserable or anxious, but once you view smiling as another tool in your anxiety toolkit, a specific anxiety-busting technique if you will, then you might feel differently about trying it.

Being negative and looking miserable is a habit and it's a good one to try and break, because it doesn't do you any good and it certainly doesn't do anyone around you any good either. If you have kids, then being a good role model and making a conscious effort to smile whenever you remember to not only makes you a nicer person to live with, it also teaches them by example. It doesn't turn you into a Pollyanna type or a naively optimistic person, it is simply choosing to smile rather than frown and laugh rather than complain.

A Daily Dose of Laughter

If smiling releases endorphins, serotonin and other good things, then imagine what laughter can do! There are so many health benefits from lowering blood pressure to boosting the immune system that it's worth taking laughter seriously.

Back in the 1960s journalist Norman Cousins was diagnosed with a fatal illness called Ankylosing Spondylitis. He tried various remedies, both conventional and alternative, but they had almost no effect on his mystifying condition. Finally, he decided to check himself out of hospital and follow his own treatment program of laughter therapy, spending his time watching TV shows like Candid Camera and comedy films. When he had his next check-up, doctors could find no trace of the disease. Cousins documented this in his 1979 book Anatomy of an Illness, which was later made into a movie. It triggered a lifelong interest in the effect of emotions on someone's biochemistry and he wrote many other books on illness and healing from the layman's perspective.

No-one is suggesting that laughter can cure serious illnesses like Ankylosing Spondylitis or cancer, but it can certainly help alleviate symptoms and counter depression and anxiety. Ten minutes of laughter can reduce stress by up to 70 percent.

There are different ways to ensure you get your daily dose. The first is to take an inventory of what really tickles your funny bone. Make a list of all the TV shows, comedians, jokes, books, cartoons and YouTube clips that have made you laugh out loud in the past, and keep the list handy. You can keep adding to it as you find new things. The point of the list is to take time every day to revisit at least one of the items on the list. I have to confess that *"Ultimate Dog Tease"* on YouTube cracks me up every single time. If you don't know it, then do a search on YouTube. You've got the right one if it mentions bacon and maple syrup. Some of my friends don't find it funny, you might not either. The point is, humor is very personal. It's your list and if it makes you laugh, then write it down.

When you are feeling very anxious or worried, you may not be able to laugh, even at the funniest videos or stories, which is where therapeutic laughter can play a role. Laughter Yoga was created in the mid-1990s by Indian medical doctor Madan Kataria and they encourage participants to *"laugh for no reason"*. to simulate laughter until the real thing kicks in. Apparently, it only takes ten minutes a day to feel a real difference. There are over 10,000 laughter yoga classes and clubs all over the world if you want to give it a go. You can type Internal Jogging (such a great title!) into YouTube to watch a short documentary about it.

You might like to try and find your own laughter role model. This could be a funny celebrity, a friend with a playful nature, or even someone like Scandinavian "Laughter Guru" Thomas Flindt, who teaches laughter to individuals and big business through workshops and yoga sessions. The companies that have participated have reported higher sales and profits since introducing the laughter therapy, plus of course their employees are happier. In his book Happy Lemons he writes: ***"Breathing and laughing are your most important energy resources. It doesn't make you feel alive, it keeps you alive."***

If you are in the habit of keeping a journal or diary, and I thoroughly recommend that you do, then make sure you note the funny stuff that happens to you every day as well as the drama.

How To Share the Fun

Have you heard of *"random acts of kindness"?* Maybe you have also heard the term *"paying it forward"?* Both of them have the same basic concept at their core, that you do a good deed for someone either because someone has done one for you or just for the sake of it. If the random act of kindness is for a stranger and is anonymous, it's even better. Now why on earth would you want to pick up the tab for the old lady sitting in the corner of the coffee shop or pay the toll on the freeway for the person behind you?

The Random Acts of Kindness Foundation has research to show that there are many positive effects to being kind, and not just for the recipients of the good deed. They cite research from Emory University concerning the *"helper's high",* an effect brought on by being kind to another person, which activates the reward and pleasure centers in the giver's brain. They also report: *"Witnessing acts of kindness produces oxytocin, occasionally referred to as the 'love hormone' which aids in lowering blood pressure and improving our overall heart health. Oxytocin also increases our self-esteem and optimism, which is extra helpful when we're anxious or shy in a social situation."*

It takes effort to do nice things, particularly if you are feeling anxious and stressed, but view it as necessary and beneficial therapy, with the added bonus of making those around you feel good. Don't reserve the random acts for strangers either. Spread the love around family, friends and acquaintances and then wallow in all the positive changes you notice in your life.

While we are on the subject of spreading the love, let's consider social media for a moment. If your Facebook and Twitter accounts are anything like mine, there will be lots of memes, videos and viral posts forwarded by friends. Many people forward things that are basically just rants or criticisms and I make it my business to delete those immediately. Life is too short to share gloomy, negative posts, is it not? On the other hand, if I receive or find something inspirational and uplifting, funny or fascinating I will forward it to friends, in the hope of at least raising a smile and creating some positive mojo. It doesn't sound that important, but as I mentioned earlier, small habits can have a big impact on your life, so you need to be aware of them and change any that aren't doing you good.

In Praise of Praise

Criticism and carping are easy. Sarcasm and sniping are easy. Misery and moaning are easy too. But praise, well now, there's a thing. A few kind words of encouragement or appreciation can go a very long way. They have the power to make someone's day and change moods in a heartbeat. I know, it's a lot simpler to say nothing to the check-out clerk or the waitress, just look down and pay up. Engagement with other people is energy-draining, especially when you are not in the mood for it. But in the light of everything else I've been saying about these activities being therapeutic, think of doling out praise as an exercise which will help you with your anxiety. It will make you feel better and will most definitely have a positive impact on the recipient.

You can always find something nice to say to a person, so start making it a habit to give compliments. Someone may have a lovely smile, or a great color of nail polish, or an infectious laugh. So, tell them, without making it sound fake or like you are coming on to them. Be genuine in your praise and don't wait for a compliment in return. Praise and run!

The Key To "Play"

As we have already discussed, mindfulness is a very good strategy for dealing with anxiety. Really focusing with intent on the here-and-now calms the mind and relaxes the body. Laughing and smiling, particularly the therapeutic rather than the spontaneous kind, can really make us concentrate on the present moment and appreciate that now is all we have.

Playing is another good example of mindfulness in action, particularly if you focus on the experience for its own sake rather than having an end goal. Children and young animals have no problem at all in doing things for the sheer fun of it, yet as adults we tend to lose that joy. Playing seems silly, pointless and makes us feel awash with guilt. Shouldn't we be working? Aren't there a million chores on our to-do list? In fact, this attitude is completely mistaken. Play is good for you, it aids creativity, helps relieve stress and anxiety and improves brain function. It triggers the release of our old friends, endorphins and can even relieve pain temporarily. Are you convinced yet?

It doesn't really matter what type of play you engage in, although I would say there was a pretty strong case for avoiding anything electronic or digital. Have a go on the swings in the park, throw a frisbee for the dog, roll down a hill like you did when you were nine, do a jigsaw or hit a tennis ball around with a friend. The most important thing is that you have some guilt-free time getting totally absorbed in something fun. It isn't selfish, and it isn't stupid. Even if you have a list of tasks as long as your arm and a load of people relying on you, you can always find fifteen minutes for fun. Remember what they tell you on aircraft about putting on your own oxygen mask first, before helping anyone else? Well, play is like your oxygen mask, because if you don't take care of yourself first, you will be in no fit state to help others, will you?

Real Life Case Study

After doing her detailed inventory, Serena now had a fairly good idea of what triggered her anxiety. She was certainly a lot more reflective and tried to make time to check how she was feeling at intervals during the day. She began looking at the anxiety as a thing she could overcome, rather than letting herself be defined by it.

She sat down one day while Amelia was taking a nap and thought about how her life and her behavior had changed. Apart from the stress and worry, she felt sad, like there was something missing in her life. When she followed this thought a little more deeply, she realized that she couldn't remember the last time she had really laughed uncontrollably or taken some time out to have fun. At work she and her friends would have what they called "mad time out" where they would all stop what they were doing and throw a paper ball around the office. If you dropped it, you had to do a forfeit. She smiled as she remembered having to talk to the sales rep from head office while standing on one leg as her colleagues smirked and made faces in the background. *"You need some fun,"* she said to herself. It was raining, but since when had that stopped her? She pulled on her jacket and rubber boots, scooped Amelia up and put her in her stroller then went outside.

Feeling a little self-conscious at first, she began jumping into the puddles in the garden, making the biggest splash she could. Then she stood in quite a big puddle and stamped her feet quickly up and down like a three-year-old. She found she was smiling at herself and she wasn't the only one. Amelia had woken up and was looking at her in amazement as was her neighbor Mrs. Harris. She waved up at her and then took Amelia for a walk, making sure she splashed wildly in each puddle on the way.

After her walk, Serena tackled some ironing while watching some episodes of **Friends** instead of the 24-hour rolling news show she usually had on. She'd forgotten how much she enjoyed it, she even found herself laughing out loud a couple of times.

She was surprised at how these two small actions lifted her mood, even temporarily. It seemed that laughter was the best medicine after all and the added bonus, given her precarious financial state, was that it didn't cost anything either.

Chapter 6 Take-aways

In this chapter we have looked at:

- The physiological effects of smiling and laughter

- The effects of smiling on others

- Norman Cousins, the man who cured himself with laughter

- How to plan a daily dose of laughter

- Therapeutic laughter and Laughter Yoga

- Random acts of kindness and paying it forward

- The power of play

When you are feeling stressed and anxious, you can often neglect your health and appearance, but looking after your body properly can help relieve some of the symptoms of stress, as you are about to find out.

Chapter 7 – How To Look After Your Body

"To keep the body in good health is a duty ... otherwise we shall not be able to keep our minds strong and clear."
Buddha

There is a strong and well-understood connection between the body and the mind, it is common sense that what affects one affects the other and yet so many times we treat them as two separate entities. We run to doctors for medicines to help us with a digestive problem or to help us sleep, focusing on the symptoms individually and expecting pills to make us better. Yet if we don't address the cause, if we don't use joined up thinking to realize that a dry mouth, aching muscles, high blood pressure, insomnia and stomach cramps could all be connected to stress, and that the cause of the stress needs to be tackled to alleviate the other symptoms, we will never truly achieve good health.

Your body is your friend. It is a finely-tuned mirror reflecting your current state of well-being, both mental and physical. Its natural state is always towards balance and health and the way it leaps into action when, for example, you get an infection or cut yourself is testament to the fact it is always ready to protect you and heal you. But if you abuse it, and by that I don't just mean in the traditional sense of drinking too much and taking hard drugs, but in a more chronic and insidious way, by regularly pumping it full of stress chemicals, not taking exercise and not eating well, it will find it increasingly difficult to do its job.

Tuning In

Do you know what worry feels like? Have you ever paid attention to what is happening in your body from the soles of your feet to the crown of your head? Don't worry, if you have never tried this then you are not alone!

Most of us pay scant attention to the micro messages our bodies send us all the time. Yes, when we get a cold, headache or a stomach upset then we take notice, but only enough to take something to make it go away. It's irritating when flu stops us from getting on with things, or a cough wakes us in the night, but apart from when things go wrong, we rarely check to see how we feel. We don't tune in, but if we did, it might make all the difference.

One of the most fundamental things you can do for your health, both physical and psychological, is to get to know your own body and how you react to both pleasant and unpleasant situations. So, let's try an experiment and see if we can begin to learn just how much information our body gives us all the time. The first part is quite unusual, in that you are going to think of something negative, but this is just to give you a benchmark. As you know, the brain doesn't distinguish between real and imagined events, which is why injured professional sports performers are often told to imagine they are doing their sport, as this *"mental work out"* has been proven to aid recovery almost as much as actual physiotherapy.

First of all, get comfortable and relaxed. Make sure you are somewhere where you won't be disturbed for about 15 minutes or so. Switch off your phone and other devices.

Close your eyes and start breathing deeply and regularly. It might help to breathe in for a count of four, hold for four and exhale for four.

Choose a situation, past, present or future, which you associate with worry and stress. Don't make this too traumatic. If you find it easier, you can think of a person who winds you up or who you strongly dislike. Try and immerse yourself in the thought, imagine you are there in the situation or with the person, see in your mind's eye what is around you and what you can hear and smell.

Now scan your body from head to toe (*or vice versa*). Notice how you feel.

Is there tension? Where is it located?

How is your breathing? *(Maybe you are holding your breath.)*
Is your mouth dry or full of saliva?
Do you feel nauseous or faint?
Really try to pay attention to your body.

Before you do the next part, use your imagination to create a good outcome to the scene you have just envisioned. If it's past, you can change history! If it's present or future, then make something nice happen. If it's a person you dislike, then imagine that they give you a present or a hug or apologize, or simply fade into the background. Close the scene on a positive note.
Now repeat the steps above, but this time put yourself in a positive situation or being with a person you really like or love.

How does your body feel now? Get used to acknowledging what a happy, relaxed feeling is like in your body. Do you feel it in a particular place? Your stomach? Your heart? There are no right or wrong answers, it's entirely personal.

Now slowly become aware of the room and your surroundings again and open your eyes. If necessary, make notes about what messages your body gave you in each situation.

Make a promise to yourself that you will tune in to your body, even if you have no symptoms, regularly during the day. Slowly, you will come to recognize how you react physically to both positive and negative situations. This can be especially useful if you have to make a decision with a few options and are not sure which one to take. Imagine the different options and pay attention to how your body reacts.

If you appreciate that certain emotions, thoughts and situations trigger physical symptoms of stress or anxiety in your body then you can take steps to deal with them. As we have already discussed, chronic stress does your body no good at all. The chemicals, like cortisol and adrenaline, that flood your system to deal with a flight-or-fight situation were designed to be short term fixes appropriate to a more primitive lifestyle, helping you to run faster or jump higher than the tiger that was chasing you. When the modern-day tiger is a traffic jam or a difficult boss and you can't hit them or run away then the stress chemicals are sloshing around with nowhere to go. The levels drop when the stress goes, but our 21st-century lifestyle means we have many stressors, so as the difficult boss walks away your computer crashes or the school calls to say your child needs to go home because they're sick … and so it goes on. We remain in a semi-stressed state of alertness almost all the time and our bodies pay the price.

Unless we decide to adopt the lifestyle of a Trappist monk or a recluse, which may not be that realistic or practical, it is hard to remove the many causes of stress in our lives. But we can learn to take note of the warning signs and then take steps to deal with the situation. One good way of doing this is through movement.

Do This! This Can Change A Lot!

Don't worry if you are not very athletically inclined, because not all movement is strenuous. The point is that movement alleviates stress because it helps get the adrenaline and cortisol levels in your body back to normal.

Walking: One of the very best ways to get a movement *"fix"* is walking. It sounds such a cliché to say, *"take the stairs not the elevator",* but it is true, there are countless opportunities around to walk if you need them. However, in this instance we are talking about moving specifically to alleviate a stressful situation, rather than a regular regime (which is also an excellent idea, of course).

So, although you could run up and down the stairs a few times, and probably get a few funny looks while doing it, the best thing to do if you feel stress building in your body to simply go out for a walk. Research conducted at Stanford and Edinburgh, has shown that walking in natural surroundings is the most beneficial, even if this a park or botanical gardens and not the countryside. In Japan there is a tradition of Shinrin-yoku, translated as *"forest bathing"* and a 2011 Japanese government study showed that subjects who walked in the forest as opposed to an urban environment had lower levels of cortisol, blood pressure and pulse rate.

When you are walking to calm yourself after a stressful situation then try not to play it over and over in your mind. As we have already seen, the brain does not distinguish between real and imagined situations and you'll just end up even more stressed! Better to try a meditative technique as you walk, such as counting your steps, or a mindfulness technique as described earlier, like really focusing on the sights, sounds and smells around you and how your body feels as you are walking.

Sex: Jumping between the sheets when you have had a stressful time is another and perhaps more appealing way to feel better. Touching and hugging your partner as well as orgasm itself has been shown to release oxytocin which is the feel-good hormone that helps to lower cortisol. There are plenty of other anti-stress benefits that sex provides, including better sleep *(thanks to the post orgasm release of the hormone prolactin),* a good pelvic floor workout for the ladies, lower blood pressure and higher levels of certain antibodies, meaning you get sick less often.

Yoga: Practicing yoga is a great way to relieve stress. If there aren't classes near you or you don't have the time or inclination to go to an organized session, then you can easily follow along with guided classes on YouTube. Apart from the general health and relaxation benefits that yoga provides, there are specific poses that are designed to be almost instant tension, stress and anxiety busters. One of these, called Vajrasana if you are interested, is very simple and very effective, so follow along!

Kneel on the ground and then sit back down on your heels. Keep your spine straight and imagine a cord running through your core and attached to the sky. Cross your arms over your chest and tuck your hands under each armpit, leaving the thumbs out and resting on the area next to your armpit. It should feel like you are almost hugging yourself. Breathe in and out with long slow breaths at least ten times.

Swimming: This is another aerobic exercise which is good at helping relieve anxiety and stress. The movements in the water helps bring the fight or flight levels down to normal, a brisk swim releases endorphins and provides a good physical workout, the rhythmic breathing and regular, repetitive movements bring on an almost hypnotic or meditative state highly conducive to relaxation. The warm water itself (assuming you don't dive into the icy waters of a frozen lake or winter ocean) can provide a feeling of safety and almost womb-like tranquility as you float blissfully around the pool.

An article in Swimmer magazine entitled Staying Happy? by Jim Thornton quotes Aimee C. Kimball, director of mental training at the Center for Sports Medicine at the University of Pittsburg Medical Center who says, *"we know ... that vigorous exercise like swimming can significantly decrease both anxiety and depression."* While Moby Coquillard, a swimmer and psychotherapist from San Mateo, California says in the same article: *"I absolutely believe swimming can serve as a kind of medicine. For me, it represents a potent adjunct to antidepressant medications and, for some patients, it's something you can take in lieu of pills."*

Running: Like swimming, running is an aerobic exercise that helps with anxiety and brings stress chemical levels in the body back to normal. It also helps with breathing, and controlling your breathing is a very important technique when learning to control anxiety and cope with panic attacks. You need to build up to running, but once you do, the beneficial effects of a good, hard run can alleviate symptoms of anxiety for hours.

Tai Chi and Qigong: These Chinese exercise systems, both derived from martial arts, are perfect for relieving stress, their soft, slow, flowing movements and regulated breathing are like doing moving meditations, as long as you don't obsess about form and instead concentrate on breathing and relaxing. As with yoga, you can join a class or find some of the free ones on YouTube. One simple exercise is the great Tai Chi Circle. Stand with your weight equally spread between your two feet and your arms loosely down by your sides. Then while breathing in, lift up your arms and draw a big circle (one side of the circle per arm). When you reach the point above your head stop and while breathing out bring your arms straight down together in front of you. It takes about 30 seconds and is highly effective.

Breathing: This Is How You Should Do It To Reduce Anxiety

When you are stressed and anxious or having a panic attack, your breathing alters. You tend to breathe from the upper chest and often feel as if you can't get enough air. Because you are taking short, shallow breaths using your chest and not your diaphragm it can lead to a tight feeling as your chest muscles tense up. This kind of breathing also makes you feel nauseous and light-headed and can make your heart beat faster and cause your hands and feet to go numb or get pins and needles. Feeling you can't breathe is scary in itself, but add the other symptoms caused by over-breathing and it is no wonder you may think you are having a heart attack and panic. The advice is usually to take deep breaths, but this can make things worse unless you do them properly.

Here are two exercises which will help you:

Breathing from your stomach: Put one hand on your chest and the other on your stomach, around your beltline. Sigh and close your mouth. Then push your stomach out which will make you inhale through your nose. Pause and then open your mouth and exhale slowly by pulling your stomach in. Repeat, all the time breathing slowly and steadily and checking you don't feel dizzy or light-headed.

The Buteyko Method: This method of breathing is quite different from the first, but try it to see if it benefits you. It was developed in the 1950s by Russian scientist Konstantin Buteyko and involves breathing *"lightly, superficially and only through the nose."* Buteyko feels that many people breathe too deeply causing them to take in too much oxygen and over dilute the amount of carbon dioxide in the blood. There are exercises online that you can watch and try for yourself, just Google *"Buteyko breathing"* or type it into YouTube. The general principal is to train yourself to only breathe through your nose and to dramatically reduce the number of breaths you take per minute. It is also said to help asthma sufferers, not just those with anxiety.

Getting Better Sleep!

Shakespeare got it right when he wrote *that "sleep knits up the ravell'd sleeve of care."* A good night's sleep has numerous health benefits, in fact, it is one of the most important things you can do for your mental and physical health. Poor sleep is linked to a variety of conditions, including inflammatory bowel disease, decreased immune function, blood sugar issues, increased risk of heart disease and stroke, lack of concentration, and reduced productivity. Ninety percent of people with depression report problems with sleep and 70 percent of those with stress and anxiety problems say they have trouble sleeping.

The ideal is eight hours, but for many this will just seem impossible. One of the most annoying things about having anxiety and worry is that it affects your sleep, making you wake up in the night or have trouble getting to sleep at all. Lack of sleep then makes you feel terrible, but no matter how tired you are you can't sleep and then you worry about not sleeping - and so the vicious circle is set.

There are ways that you can optimize your chances of getting a good night's sleep:

- Eat the right *"sleep-inducing"* foods. These will often include tryptophan, melatonin or magnesium, all of which help induce sleep, or chemicals such as calcium, which help in their absorption or production. Foods include: turkey, walnuts, pistachio nuts, cherry juice, honey, kale, shrimp, banana, Marmite and hummus.

- Have a sleep routine, this trains your mind to expect to go to bed and go to sleep after following certain rituals, for example having a bath, having a milky drink then going to bed at 10.30.

- Don't have any electronic devices in the bedroom. TVs, smart phones, laptop, tablet – all a big no as far as sleep is concerned.

- Try bathing in a bath with Epsom Salts or massaging your stomach with magnesium oil as both contain magnesium, a very good sleep-inducer.

- Don't eat a meal or drink alcohol for a few hours before sleeping.

- Try herbal tablets such as valerian (an ancient sleep remedy) or tablets with melatonin in them.

- Keep your bedroom dark and cool. (Cool in the temperature sense, that is!)

+ Make sure you are physically tired, so try to go outdoors, exercise or have a long walk during the day.

- Don't *"saw sawdust"*. Leave the day's troubles behind you, imagine throwing them in the bin or having them written on a sheet of paper and turning the paper over. The point is, the day is over, and you don't want to spend the night reliving things you can do nothing about.

- Investigate some of the very good sleep hypnosis or guided meditation videos on YouTube. Plug in your earphones, close your eyes and you'll be asleep before you know it.

Looking After Yourself

You must learn to be your own best friend and fiercest advocate, therefore you need to have some little treats which needn't cost the earth but can make you feel pampered and spoilt. One common symptom of depression is self-neglect, but it's amazing how much of a boost something as simple as wearing a different color or having a new hairstyle can be. These little treats needn't cost the earth or be complicated either. A nice soak in the bath with some bath oil or bubble bath is relaxing and indulgent without being expensive. Listening to your favorite music, watching a good movie, buying yourself some flowers or a lovely box of chocolates or treating yourself to a magazine or a good book are great ways to spoil yourself too. Remember, it's a personal thing, you know best what makes you feel good. Have some fun and make a list of your top ten treats, then make an effort, even if you don't feel like it, to incorporate at least one treat into every day.

Of course, if you want to push the boat out a bit then a massage or spa treatment or a makeover can really make you feel special. And you can look after your body in a different way by planning a lovely meal in your favorite restaurant or buy a bottle of your favorite wine. The point is, it should move you from the mundane to the extraordinary, it should lift your spirits and make you smile. And why not? You deserve it!

Chapter 7 Takeaways

In this chapter we have looked at:

- The mind/body connection

- How to tune into your body in both positive and negative situations

- Different ways to destress using movement and exercise

- The importance of how you breathe and two breathing techniques

- The power of sleep and different ways to ensure you get your full quota

- Some important ways to pamper yourself

In the next chapter we are going to look at the other vital aspect of your own wellbeing, your mind and how you can best use it to conquer anxiety and worry. So, let's find out more!

Chapter 8 – Easily Harnessing The Power of your Mind

"The energy of the mind is the essence of life."
Aristotle

Your mind is the most powerful tool you possess. It governs everything, how you perceive and process information, how you react to things, what you feel, what you think. It is the source of your imagination, your creativity and your dreams. Even your five senses are processed in your mind. Your nose may be the thing that does the sniffing but it's your mind that decodes the smell!

Deciding to learn more about your how your mind works and to take control of your thoughts is one of the most important things you can ever do, a gift to yourself. Yet the vast majority of people will never bother to do this and will spend most of their lives *"asleep"*, not aware of just what they could achieve if they decided to master their thinking.

So, first of all, you should congratulate yourself on being interested enough to get this far. You are already in the minority. You already have a huge advantage over most people. The mind is truly incredible and the more you learn about it, the more you will appreciate just how it can help you not only overcome anxiety and worry, but also give you the confidence to build the life you deserve.

Here are a few facts about the mind that may surprise you and, I hope, fill you with appreciation for the powerhouse between your ears.

- According to latest estimates we have 86 billion brain cells.

- We each have about 50,000 thoughts per day. However, it's been estimated about 70 percent of this mind talk is negative! *(Self-criticism, anxiety and so on.)*

- There are about 400 miles of blood vessels in the brain.

- Your brain can change and develop new cells throughout your lifetime.

- The memory capacity of the brain is 1015 bytes - the same as the whole World Wide Web.

- The human brain is 30 times more powerful than some of the world's fastest supercomputers.

- About 95 percent of decisions happen in your subconscious mind.

- You have "secondary brains" in your intestines (100 million neurons) and your heart (about 40,000 neurons), which throws light on the expression "gut feeling" and may also explain why many heart transplant subjects take on the memory and personality of their donors.

There are many, many more facts about your brain than those, and if you are interested you can research it in Google. But what I hope you get from this is just how complex and truly incredible the mind is, yet we are never taught how to use it properly. I certainly never had a *"user's manual"* when I was in school.

You Are What You Think

The mind can be your best friend, but it can be your worst enemy too. Shakespeare put it very well when he wrote: *"There is nothing either good or bad, but thinking makes it so."* The poet John Milton echoed this when he wrote: *"The mind is its own place and in itself can make a Heaven of Hell, a Hell of Heaven."*

The mind plays a big role in stress or worry, and you can literally think yourself into, and out of, a panic state. This is not to apportion blame. Don't feel that your anxiety is a figment of your imagination. The fears and symptoms are very real, and it is not your fault if you feel this way. The important thing now is to understand the role of the mind in anxiety and stress, and help harness its power in a positive way to help you feel better.

If you have heard the expression a *"self-fulfilling prophecy"* then you will know that people very often get what they expect, good or bad. I have a friend who is very loyal and kind to her family and close friends, but thinks strangers are out to cheat her and can't be trusted. She believes that *"you should kick dirt in people's faces before they kick dirt in yours."* Of course, this isn't true, but she approaches every transaction with this attitude and treats people in an aggressive and distrustful way that doesn't bring out the best in those she is dealing with. They can feel her hostility and dislike and are therefore defensive in their responses. The result is that everything gets off on the wrong foot and often degenerates from there, which leads her to say, *"You see, I told you they couldn't be trusted!"*

Research has discovered that we use the same part of the brain to think about the past and the future. That's why we tend to anticipate the outcome of future events based on past experience. If you lost your way when driving in a new place then you will understandably feel anxious that the same thing will happen again next time you drive somewhere you aren't familiar with. The degree of anxiety will reflect what happened in the past, so if you once got lost in a snowstorm at night then this will have more of an impact than making a wrong turn on a spring day.

Add to this the fact that your mind loves having *"little chats"* with you, often fear-inducing or negative, and you can see how a scenario could build up: *"Oh, so you have to drive to Fairfield for the job interview? Well you don't know where that is, do you? We all know how great you are at directions, so you're bound to get lost. It'll be like West Hampton all over again! Weather looks bad too, it'll probably snow or rain, knowing your luck. It's going to take hours to get there too, especially if you take a wrong turning, which you will, so it'll be dark. You know how bad you are at driving in the dark. Actually, you're pretty bad at driving, period, aren't you? Probably best not to go. You won't get the job anyway. Remember the last time? ..."*

Sound familiar? We all do this to some extent, but if you suffer from anxiety, you do it more than most. The good news is that there are ways to counter it. Awareness is key. Understanding what is going on and why your mind is doing this is half the battle. You may not be able to stop the memories of a negative situation or the stream of chatter in your head, but you can choose not to react to it.

Taking Control

Mastering your thoughts and your inner chatter is an ongoing process and you need to check in a lot to make sure you are on top of things. The steps you take are not that hard, but as the saying goes: *"it's simple, but it's not easy"*.

Your mind is constantly at work. A lot of what it does is to screen information so that you don't get overwhelmed with the millions of messages your brain takes in every day. It sorts out the relevant from the inconsequential and draws things to your attention that you have indicated are important. This may be something you have been focusing on. For example, if you wanted to buy a blue dress for a wedding you then start seeing blue dresses everywhere. There aren't any more blue dresses than before, it's just that you have sent your brain the message that you are now interested in them, so what is called the reticular activation system no longer ignores them but highlights them for you instead.

That is all well and good for innocuous things like blue dresses, but if you constantly fret over negative things and reinforce them by focusing on them all the time, then your brain will still do its thing and bring examples to your attention because it thinks that they are important to you. A friend of mine Robin lives in California. She is constantly thinking about earthquakes. Now, residents of California know that there are sensible precautions to take when you live in an earthquake zone: knowing the safest spot in a building, having an emergency bag packed and so on, but Robin takes this a lot further.

She follows stories about earthquakes from anywhere in the world in the news and social media *(there's always an earthquake happening somewhere)* and regularly visits an earthquake reporting website. She won't put any pictures up in her rented apartment in case they get damaged when they fall off the walls when the earthquake hits.

She is a little bit obsessed by earthquakes and because she spends such a lot of time thinking about them, her brain has made the understandable assumption that earthquakes are important to her and so flags up lots of earthquake-related things all the time. I remember being with her at the airport and she dragged me half way across the shopping center to a bookstall where she had somehow, from many feet away, spotted a book about earthquakes on sale. I hadn't even noticed the bookstall! She lives her life in a constant state of anxiety and fuels her fears by feeding them.

This is an extreme example, but you get the point. You can turn your everyday life into a negative and pretty scary place if you constantly focus on the bad things about the world and about yourself. Fortunately, the opposite is also true. In his book ***The Luck Factor: The Scientific Study of the Lucky Mind***, British psychologist Professor Richard Wiseman decided to make a scientific investigation of just what makes some people luckier than others. He placed ads in the press asking people to contact him if they thought they were extremely lucky or extremely unlucky. He then did a detailed analysis of the lives of the 400 volunteers from all walks of life who contacted him over the years. Some really did appear exceptionally lucky or unlucky. Wiseman asked them to write diaries, fill in questionnaires, be interviewed and take part in experiments. After all these years of research this is what he concluded: *"...lucky people generate their own good fortune via four basic principles. They are skilled at creating and noticing chance opportunities, make lucky decisions by listening to their intuition, create self-fulfilling prophesies via positive expectations, and adopt a resilient attitude that transforms bad luck into good."*

Wiseman's conclusions are very encouraging. He states that you can learn to be lucky. In fact, in the book he describes how he started a Luck School, training the self-confessed unlucky people how to attract greater good fortune with often startling results. What can we learn from this to help overcome anxiety and worry? Let's look at a few ideas from the book.

Shake things up a bit. Lucky people tend to deliberately break their routines and introduce variety. If they feel they are getting into a rut, then they will deliberately attempt to change their behavior. This makes sense because repeating familiar routines blinds you to them. You are far more likely to notice opportunities in unfamiliar surroundings because you are having to pay attention and be mindful of what's happening. In the same way, to stop hanging out with the same group of people, do something that will force you to meet new ones. Wiseman describes how one of the participants in the book decides only to talk to people wearing a particular color at a party, for example.

Thank your lucky stars. Not all of life is sunshine and roses, even lucky people have bad things happen to them. The trick is in how you deal with the crap! Rather than look at the glass half empty, try the opposite. If someone bumps into your car and makes a small dent in the door, then make an effort to be grateful it wasn't something more expensive and more serious, rather than focusing on how unlucky you were to be in the wrong place at the wrong time and why does this always happen to you? Yes, it takes practice to look at things this way, but it is worth it.

Dear Diary, Guess What Happened?: Every evening, write down all the lucky and positive things that have happened to you each day, no matter how small. Even if you found a cent on the ground, write it in your diary! Read the list from the previous day before adding today's events. As the list builds and you start appreciating the number of good things happening to you, you will begin to focus on that and not the bad.

There are some other techniques you can use to master your thoughts and feel less anxious. One of the most straightforward is to observe your own mind at work. Become aware of what you are thinking and just observe without judgement. The only requirement is to notice. You don't criticize, you just start paying attention to how that gray matter between your ears is working. Is it wandering? Is it focused?

Is it regurgitating old worries and playing back long-gone scenarios? Watch your thoughts as they come and go.

If you really want to go really deep, then think about this. When you notice *"Ah, I'm feeling quite anxious at the moment and I'm thinking a lot about what might happen tonight,"* which part of you is noticing that? Which part of your mind is stepping back and observing? Interesting, huh?

Now imagine that you can enter into the space between thoughts, the space where that observer lives. What would that be like? Can you feel, even for a second, what it is like in that perfect and peaceful space? A space without thoughts? A space to just be? Even trying to do this for a short time, or thinking about this space, will create an awareness that you are not your thoughts. Your thoughts run through your mind, but they are not who you are.

The Steps To Reframing Your Thoughts

There is a way that you can change how you react to and interpret something negative that is happening or has happened to you. It's called reframing. Our negative thoughts are not helpful and it is worth learning how to recalibrate them in order to feel happier.

It should now be obvious that many of your thoughts are a product of your experience, beliefs and assumptions. Something happens, but that event in itself is neutral. It is only our interpretation of it that gives it significance. This is not in any way to downplay tragedy, but even there, good can come out of disaster. Different people can view the same situation and be affected in profoundly different ways, depending on the way they think, what they believe and their own life history. For example, a snowstorm causes one person to panic because she hates driving in snow but has to get to work, a child to clap their hands in excitement as they think about a day off school and building a snowman, the CEO of a salt company to smile at his increased profits as he sends out extra supplies to the highway companies and a young man to start crying as he remembers how his late Mom used to love the snow. You see how we can interpret things differently?

Once you are aware that events are in themselves neutral and that your thoughts are shaping your interpretation, even if this is to try and help or protect you, then you can try reframing them. Here is one way:

- Think of a situation that affects you in a negative way

- Try and work out how you are framing it. What is making you view it so negatively? Is it because of certain limiting beliefs you hold? A past experience? A set of beliefs that may not even be yours? Old fears and phobias?

- If the situation is a learning experience, what is it teaching you?

- What advice would you give to a friend looking at the situation in the same way?

- What kind of language are you using in your self-talk about this situation? Can you tone it down a bit? Instead of saying *"I really, really hate going to parties,"* could you say, *"parties are not my favorite way to spend time, but they can sometimes be fun."*

- Can you set yourself a bit of a challenge? If you find you are reacting to a situation based on old programming or conditioning, then how could you look at it differently. Instead of saying *"I'm wasting my life, I don't even know what job I want to do, I'm just a jack-of-all-trades-master-of-none..."* like your dad used to say to you, then why not challenge your assumptions and reframe your thoughts. Is what you are thinking true? Really? Is not wanting to focus on one thing as a career a bad thing?

Many of the world's geniuses, like Leonardo da Vinci, were multi-talented. Also, these days, people no longer have jobs for life. In the 21st century a *"portfolio career"* is common. You are very lucky to have the opportunity to try out some different things, hey, you could even combine your skills into a new and fascinating business that has never been done before. It's an incredible opportunity to make the most of your individuality and unique abilities.

There are many more ways to help you tame the incredible but sometimes unruly creature that is your mind, but just start with these ideas, even just one of them and you have already taken huge strides. Well done.

Chapter 8 Takeaways

In this chapter we have learned:

- How amazing your mind is and what astounding feats it is capable of

- How it can be a two-edged sword, making you fearful and anxious or positive and motivated

- That you use the same part of the brain to look at the past and the future

- That mastering your mind is an essential life skill

- Your mind will bring to your attention things you regularly focus on, whether blue dresses or earthquakes

- People can learn to make their own luck

- You can use various techniques, including reframing, to begin to manage your mind rather than have it manage you.

Next, we are going to look at one of the most exciting areas of all (see how you are already getting excited. And you don't even know what it is yet!) We are going to dive into the magic waters of creativity. Hold onto your hat!

Chapter 9 - Creativity Is Key

"Imagination is the beginning of creation. You imagine what you desire, you will what you imagine, and at last, you create what you will."
George Bernard Shaw

There are many ways to tackle anxiety and stress and we have looked at a few of them in this book. But a neglected area is creativity, because it's something people often associate with actors, artists, musicians and writers. They believe that you have to have an outstanding talent or a brilliant idea to practice creativity. That is so mistaken! Every one of us is creative, it is as much a part of us as breathing or eating, we just forget sometimes how to let it come through.

Creativity is very helpful with anxiety and stress. By placing your focus on something you are making or doing, your mind is taken away from problems and worry. Recent research has shown that doing something artistic reduces the level of cortisol in your body. Getting *"in the flow"*, that feeling of being completely absorbed in what you are doing so that you lose track of time, releases dopamine and serotonin. As we know by now, reducing the stress chemicals and increasing the feel-good ones is a positive thing. As if that wasn't enough, another set of research has linked creativity and longevity. Scientists studied the records of a group of 1000 people covering two decades and discovered the more creative ones lived longer.

Creativity Easily Explained

So, what exactly is creativity? Cambridge Dictionary defines it as *"the ability to produce original and unusual ideas or to make something new or imaginative."* I think that definition contains a key nugget: *"to make something new or imaginative."* My personal definition of creativity is to produce something by the end of the day that wasn't there at the beginning. It doesn't matter if it's coloring in, cake making or composing a song. The end result is a design, a donut or a ditty. In other words, something that didn't exist before you metaphorically, or literally, got your hands dirty!

People mix up creativity and ability. There is a common misconception that creative things have to be brilliant, that they could be sold for a king's ransom. This is nonsense. First of all, beauty is in the eye of the beholder. If you love it, that's good enough. If someone else loves it, terrific, but you are not doing this for other people, you're doing it for you. Secondly, unless you are an artist *(and I use the term in its widest sense)* by profession, you are not going to sell your work. In fact, you may not even show it to other people, although you can if you feel so inclined, because it's not about producing a piece that is good enough to make a living from or to be exhibited, it is about self-expression and the joy of the act itself. I repeat, you are doing this for you.

So many people have hang ups about their self-expression. *"Oh, I'm useless, I'm not at all creative. I can't draw to save my life."* There are many, many ways to be creative and it really doesn't matter if the way you express your personal creativity isn't on a particular list of traditional creative pursuits. Although we have looked at one definition, creativity doesn't have to follow a special format or tick boxes or be recognized by society. That's the whole point. It can be anything you want it to be. If, when you are out for a walk in the woods, you decide to make a heart shape on the ground from some pebbles, that is creative. If you arrange a few objects on a shelf in a way you find pleasing, that is creative. If you suddenly find a few words arranging themselves in your mind to make a funny rhyme, that is creative. If you dance around the room when you hear a favorite song, that is creative. And in case you are ready to catch me out by saying *"but a dance doesn't produce a new object by the end of the day, so it can't be creative,"* you are wrong!

A creative innovation can be ephemeral. A dance creates a pattern in space and time that wasn't there before. It shifts energy and moves molecules. Just because you can't hold a dance in your hand doesn't mean you haven't produced anything imaginative. Think about music. If you go to a live performance as each note is sung or played it disappears, but it was a creative act, even if you can't physically touch it. Are you convinced yet?

Some Easy Ways To Be More Creative

Don't feel constrained by a list, but I'm going to include one because I want to show that there are many, many ways to express your creativity and you may find something here that you did as a child and have forgotten about, or that you haven't tried but would quite like to have a go at. Feel free to dabble, doodle and dance! Add to the list if you want.

Writing – a poem, a diary entry, a story, a play, a song, your biography, your grandparents' biography, a new name for something, a joke. You can even think about the physical act of writing and try calligraphy. There are some truly inspirational calligraphers on Instagram and YouTube.

Art – painting, doodling, drawing, coloring in (some of those adult coloring books or apps are great), making collages or treasure maps, drawing a cartoon, sculpting a dragon or a daisy from clay or stone, painting stones (why not!), designing a tattoo, making a birthday card, icing a cake.

Music – singing, drumming, humming, playing the piano or penny whistle, whistling (even if out of tune), bell ringing, filling bottles with water and making a tune (I don't know if that even has a name! I expect it does.) Composing on the trombone or on your tablet (there are apps).

Crafts – weaving, knitting, crochet (all very cool at the moment, how our grannies would laugh!), origami, quilt-making, robot-making (why not!), woodworking, pottery, straw dolly making, macramé, felting, sculpting, lace making, putting a ship in a bottle, making jewelry, flower arranging, jam making, making a campfire or fashioning a shelter from branches and bracken. Building a box girder bridge or a castle from Lego, or for real!

Performing – reciting Shakespeare or your child's poem, playing charades or taking the lead in the local amateur dramatics group, improvising, doing magic tricks, telling jokes, dancing and gymnastics, performing a mime or being a film extra. Acting as if you were confident and worry-free. (I thought I would throw that in to see if you were paying attention!)

Interior and Exterior Design – painting a wall, papering a hall, moving furniture around, making a path or a secret garden, creating a focal point, learning Feng Shui, planning a vegetable patch, grouping all your ornaments into interesting patterns. Experimenting with crystals, playing with color and light and pattern inside and outside your home.

This Can Really Reduce Your Anxiety & Stress

One of the reasons for the list above was to start you thinking about the kinds of creative pursuits that interest you. Don't think of this as wasted time or energy. Deciding to pursue personal creativity is one of the most valuable and helpful things you can do to tackle your anxiety. Although we are approaching it in a light-hearted way, please take it seriously. You are a creative being and need to express it. No-one will judge you. And in case you think you are a rational, scientific and logical person who *"isn't creative"* because that is for hippies and Bohemians, think again.

Everyone, and I mean *everyone*, needs to exercise their imagination and stretch their creative muscles. Almost all the world's great discoveries were made by people playing around with ideas, theories and objects. Very often the big breakthroughs in science were made during *"down time"*. Don't feel you aren't creative – you just haven't found your special niche yet. Maybe you have to invent one of your own!

If you are feeling a bit uninspired, then think back to when you were a kid. What did you enjoy doing? What did you always want to do but weren't allowed to? What did you long to try but felt you weren't good enough? There's usually something there that will ring a bell.

Sometimes the creativity needs a little kick start, so have the materials ready. Often the thought of getting things out or preparing to be creative seems a bit onerous. So, buy, paper, pens, crayons, glue, wool, whatever you are drawn to. Keep them near to hand. Then just pick something up and play around. It's important not to feel pressured into being creative, it should be natural and fun. Don't feel you have to label it or justify it. If you fancy beachcombing then just do it! It doesn't matter if it's considered a traditionally creative pursuit or not. Follow your instinct!

Your subconscious will start making suggestions or bringing things to your attention once you decide to allow this back into your life. You will be amazed how many resources there are online. There are free classes you can try, videos on YouTube, articles and magazines. There's never been an easier time to explore a variety of different hobbies on a sort of "suck it and see" basis. There are also lots of classes and groups offline, probably many in your local area. If you fancy giving one a try, then go along. Most of them will be more than happy to let you have a trial lesson or attend a session to see if you like it.

If you are really stuck for ideas, then you can decide to adopt a radical approach and try the first creative activity that you see that day. *(As long as it doesn't involve buying expensive equipment or joining a six-month long course.)* A friend of mine did this a few years ago and ended up in a woodcarving class making spoons! He loved it and has continued to *"whittle"* ever since. He says he would never have thought of working with wood before, and he only went along because it was literally the first *"creative hobby"* ad he saw that day on his way to work.

The Time For Change

If you are not used to doing something imaginative or creative on a regular basis then you will have to deliberately timetable it into your day. This may seem odd or self-indulgent or even impossible. If you are a busy mother with a million things to do, for example, then setting aside some personal time may seem like a pipe dream. But look at it like this. You are reading this book because you are struggling with anxiety. You want things to improve and to take back control of your life. At the moment, you might be operating on less than full energy. You will feel better and so will those around you if you look after yourself and your own needs and learn to relax and enjoy life again. If that means planning in a 15-minute creative space every day, then so be it. You need it.

It really doesn't have to take up a lot of time every day, the important thing is to make this a new habit. As things progress, you will find time stretches and that you move other things around, even drop other activities, so that you can spend more time just paddling around in this artistic pool. It won't take long for you to feel the benefit. But as a start, you must make that decision. *"I am going to do something creative every day."*

Be flexible in your thinking. You can do everyday chores in a creative way, it doesn't just have to be time devoted to a hobby. So, when you are cooking or cleaning or ironing, look at ways to turn that into an exercise of imagination and fun. Remember in the last chapter we learned that lucky people shook things up and avoided ruts and routine? Try doing the same with the chores you have to do. Use a different hand, start in a different place, look up some hacks on the Internet and see if they work … even the mundane can become an adventure if you are determined enough.

An Added Bonus

If the craft you decide to follow involves making something, then an added bonus is that you may find you actually like the stuff you make and want to do something with it. That is not to place any pressure on you at all. This is not a push to start a business or rent a gallery. It is the process that is important, perhaps more important than the end result. But for some people, that end result may be something you are quite proud of. In that case, you may find some options open up for you.

You can give away what you make as highly original gifts for friends and family. You just can't beat homemade and hand crafted. Speaking from experience, your efforts will be especially appreciated by people who make things themselves as they understand how much effort has gone into creating something.

You may decide to wear or showcase your creations. It is extremely satisfying to get complimented on something that you have made yourself, both offline and online on Instagram, for example. It is a real achievement to have produced something from scratch and you can be rightly proud of what you have achieved.

If they are of good standard and seem to be desirable, then you may decide to sell your things on a craft site like *Etsy*. It could lead to a money-spinning sideline or even a change in career direction, who knows?

Wherever creativity takes you, it is an exciting journey and apart from the boost to your confidence and self- esteem, time spent this way is a good antidote for anxiety and worry.

Real Life Case Study

Serena was starting to feel that she could cope more with her anxiety. She was aware of her triggers and was building regular *"fun"* times into her daily routine. She hadn't splashed about in puddles again, but that one time had done the trick, she understood how making the effort to do certain things could have a positive impact on how she felt. She was watching a lot less news and a lot more comedy shows.

After reading about the positive effects of the creative process, Serena decided she wanted to add that to her daily routine. The trouble was, she had no idea what activity to pursue. She had never thought of herself as a particularly creative person. She could knit and crochet and sew, but didn't particularly enjoy them much, perhaps because she'd been forced to do them at school. Nope, it would have to be something else. She sat for a moment, pen in hand, ready to write a list. She had read through the list in this chapter, but nothing really rang any bells or pushed any of her buttons. She decided what was needed was some visualization work. She was convinced her subconscious could help and give her an indication of what to do. She waited until Amelia was asleep, then sat down in a comfortable position and did some regular deep breathing, in for a count of six, hold for a count of six, out for a count of six and then asked her intuition to show her an image of the best creative activity to benefit her the most at this stage in her life. Serena was surprised to get an image of a church window with all its beautiful colors.

Rather than try to analyze immediately what it meant, she allowed the visualization to continue and was shown a different window, again with luminous colors. She relaxed breathed deeply and allowed her awareness to come back into the room. She checked Amelia was still fine and sleeping peacefully and then sat and reflected on the two images that she had seen. She knew they were stained glass windows. Stained glass? Was that it? She frowned for a moment, something was ringing a bell. The local free newspaper? Was that it? She retrieved this week's copy from the garbage and slowly leafed through the pages. There she found what her subconscious had been alerting her to. A beginner's course on stained glass, enrolling this Friday.

To cut a long story short, Serena enrolled on the course. They allowed her to take Amelia with her and so over a few weeks she learned how to make a simple plant holder from stained glass. Although she had never done anything like it before and always associated stained glass with churches *(hence the visualization)* Serena discovered the wealth of possibilities open to her using this amazing medium. When she was working, piecing together the different colored glass and planning the design she found that her attention was completely absorbed and she forgot all about her anxiety for the entire time she was in the class and a couple of hours after that. The moment she held her first piece in her hands she felt the most tremendous sense of achievement and satisfaction. The *"not very creative"* person had shown a surprising affinity for this unusual craft.

Chapter 9 Take-aways

In this chapter we have looked at:

- How creativity helps with anxiety and stress

- What creativity actually is

- The fact that creativity does not have to earn money or be something you can hold in your hand

- Different ways to be creative

- How to discover your own creativity

- The importance of making time to get creative

- Some other benefits

- Serena's experience in the case study.

So far, we have examined how you can take things into your own hands and do some practical exercises to alleviate anxiety. In our final chapter we do the reverse and examine how handing things over to a *"Higher Power"* might be the answer. So let's see.

Chapter 10 - Handing Things Over

"All shall be well, and all manner of things shall be well."
Julian of Norwich

In this book you have been asked to take action, learn more, or make decisions about your anxiety. But this final chapter is different. We are going to consider the consequences of believing that you can hand over the problem to a *higher power*.

What you understand by higher power is very personal. According to some polls, around 80 percent of the world's population say religion or their faith plays an important part of their lives. Some scientists also believe that the human brain is *"hardwired"* for spiritual belief. But you don't have to practice a specific religion to believe that there is a powerful energy outside yourself. Whether you call it God, the Universe, Mother Earth, All That Is or even The Force, it doesn't really matter, that should be very clear. I am not advocating you must follow traditional religion here.

It can be tremendously reassuring to feel that something, or someone, bigger than ourselves is there to share the burden and listen to our problems. Sometimes it's so tiring trying to be strong and brave and positive that it's little wonder the saying *"let go and let a higher"* is such a popular one.

Let's look at that expression for a moment. Does believing in God or the Universe mean sitting back and doing nothing and simply hoping that someone else would just come in and take over? I would answer that by reminding you of the old joke.

A man is sitting on the roof of his house, surrounded by flood water. A neighbor rows by in a small boat. *"Get out while you can!"* he shouts. *"There's space in my boat."* The man waves him away.

"God will save me," he says. An inflatable lifeboat pulls up next. *"Jump in,"* they cry. *"No, don't worry,"* replies the man, *"God will save me."*

So, the lifeboat speeds away. Next comes a helicopter. *"We'll send a rope down, grab hold of it and we'll winch you up,"* they shout. *"I don't need a rope,"* shouts back the man. *"God is going to save me."* So, the helicopter flies off. The waters get higher and higher and finally the man screams *"God! I thought you would save me! Where are you?"* A booming voice replies: *"I sent your neighbor, a lifeboat and a helicopter, what more do you want me to do?"*

Very funny, isn't it? And as with all the best jokes, there's a lot of truth in it. When faced with a problem, you can't just sit back, do nothing and expect a higher power to swoop in and rescue you. You have to make some kind of effort yourself, you have to be aware of opportunities and solutions, because often they are all around you, if you just look. And help, when it comes, is not necessarily in the form you are expecting either. You have to be open to everything, not just what your preconceived ideas tell you. In other words, the higher power has your back, but expects you to do your bit too, at least that's my take on it.

It Can Help, If You Let It

Scientific research has shown that people with a spiritual or religious belief are less anxious and can cope better with stressful situations. The power of prayer is positive too. In a book by Larry Dossey called Prayer is Good Medicine he says: *"More than 130 controlled laboratory studies show, in general, that prayer or prayer like states of compassion, empathy and love can bring helpful changes in many types of living things, from humans to bacteria. This does not mean prayer always works, any more than drugs or surgery always works but that, statistically speaking, prayer is effective."*

An important caveat here is that you must never think your anxiety is caused by *"sin"*, failing to go to church, not believing in God or not following a religion. You should not feel guilty or think that this is some kind of punishment. Some religious practices can make you feel like this. If that is the case I would suggest that you keep going on your spiritual quest, but look for a path that is more positive and supportive. Also, there are no quick fixes and easy answers. A faith will not magically make you feel better. But having hope for the future and knowing you are being cared for and loved will make a difference in your life.

Deciding What You Need

These days it seems you can almost pick and mix spiritual traditions to find the best one to fit you. The Internet and social media have helped shape this, although it has its roots a few decades ago with the rise in popularity of the New Age movement. But there is a downside to this. Too many options can be confusing, leading to paralysis of choice. It is a good thing, in any area of life, to drill down and focus, to go deep.

Although there is lots of information online, including quizzes to find out the form of spirituality that best fits you *(take a look at Beliefnet),* this is such an important issue that it is probably best to talk it through with a really good and impartial friend *(not one who is fixated on any one practice)* or a spiritual advisor. A good priest, for example, although they will inevitably want you to follow their own religious practice, should be able to give you honest and impartial advice about the options open to you, so if you know a spiritual advisor, even if not of your religion, then ask if you can have a chat. The point is that you need to talk to someone honest who will not be pushing a weird practice or cult or their own agenda.

There are different types of spiritual paths open to you, from simply being in nature and communing with the earth to yoga to a more conventional religion, like Christianity or Judaism, which may have within it various traditions from very liberal to more orthodox. It is a very personal thing, some people prefer to have more rules to follow and a very clear and organized system of worship, others prefer a freer approach. There is something out there which will speak to you, but if you find it then explore it deeply and seriously. Give it a chance to work, don't flit from one spiritual practice to another like a butterfly.

Exploring Alternatives

Deciding *"there must be more to life than this"* is a very common and important feeling. Many, many people are investigating different aspects of their own spirituality, because it is a fundamental part of being human. We crave this knowledge. Some can spend a lifetime seeking it.

It is important to say that the search itself is a valid and calming exercise. Reading books about different aspects of spirituality, watching videos, going to talks, chatting with friends - just learning more about something which is a part of everyday life and yet so different from our mundane day-to-day tasks is a wonderful and fulfilling way to spend your time.

It is often said that the spiritual path is like going on a spiral path up a mountain. You go round and round and end up in the same place, except that each time you are a bit higher up!

If you are feeling confused on your search, not sure if you should return to your own childhood faith, go New Age, become a Buddhist or a Druid, and you have tried the suggestions of talking to a trusted friend or spiritual advisor from a mainstream organization, then one thing that can help you is to access your own subconscious. We have talked about this before. Just as dreams can be an insight into how you are feeling about a situation or problem, so can some forms of guided visualization or meditation.

When asking your subconscious to help you, it is very important to phrase your question clearly. Sit down quietly and have a pen and paper to hand. Think about the issue you would like guidance about. In this case, a good question could be: Which spiritual discipline is best for me to help with my overall wellbeing and as an aid to anxiety?

If you are weighing up two or three options, then think clearly about what those options are and what you want to know. For example: I am considering Wicca, Druidry and Celtic Christianity. Please show me which would help me most in terms of my wellbeing and peace of mind.

Once you are clear on your question, then you can try to get an answer. Here are three possible methods to experiment with. If you feel you need to then you can say a short prayer beforehand asking God or Spirit to guide you and protect you and to bring you the wisest answer for your good and the good of all concerned. Even though you are accessing your subconscious mind, it may make you feel better knowing you are protected. Another way of doing this is to imagine yourself inside a sphere of pure, white light which will protect you throughout the process.

Asking for Help

An alternative to going within and asking your Higher Self or subconscious for help, is to allow the environment around you to answer your question. This can be through a random event, a book falling off a shelf, a leaflet through your letterbox, overhearing a snatch of conversation, unexpectedly finding an unusual object or something else. If you choose to use this method then two things are important, apart from, as always, clearly stating the question you want guidance about.

Firstly, you must set a clear time limit, for example: the next three hours, by 8pm tonight, by tomorrow at 10am. Secondly, you mustn't try too hard. Don't look for a sign. The sign will appear and catch you by surprise. If you find you are seeing signs everywhere and struggling with what they might mean, then they aren't signs! A true sign is clear and unequivocal - and unexpected.

The search for something bigger than ourselves, something that gives us hope and reassurance, is one of the most worthwhile things we can ever undertake. It will help you with your anxiety and in addition, give you much more to enhance every aspect of your life.

Chapter 10 Takeaways

In this chapter we have looked at:

- How many people are on a spiritual search

- That you shouldn't just sit back and expect to be rescued, you need to take action

- How spirituality can help with anxiety

- How to find the right path for you

- The option of returning to your faith

- Different ways to explore alternatives

- Three ways to access inner guidance

- Getting an answer from your environment

Conclusion: Starting Again

"Your positive action combined with positive thinking results in success."
Shiv Khera

Well, we have a come a long way together, so thank you for reading this. I hope that the book has helped you in some way towards coping with your anxiety and stress. It is not pleasant to live life in a state of fear and you now know that there are steps you can take to help yourself. I hope you will try some of them.

If you find that your days are overwhelmingly dark and you can't see a way forward, I would encourage you to seek professional help. There is no shame in it and advice and exercises in a book like this can only go so far. For depressive illnesses you need more than I can give you and there is so much that can be done these days to help you cope and recover.

If you have approached this with an open mind and an open heart, then you will have learned some practical strategies to cope. You are not alone, remember. Whether it is a friend, a colleague, a family member, a spiritual advisor or a Higher Power – *you are never alone*. You are valuable and you are loved. Don't forget it.

I know you can do this. So, to quote our lovely Shakespeare for the final time, *"screw your courage to the sticking place"* and turn towards tomorrow with a warm glow in your heart. We're all rooting for you.

Good luck and here's to a bright and positive future filled with wonderful experiences and adventures.

Thank you so much for checking out my book.

I sincerely hope you got value from it. I hope it allows you to make important changes in your life. I hope this book helps you decrease your anxiety and increase your happiness.

If you liked this book could you possibly taking 60 seconds to write a quick review on Amazon?

Reviews are a vital way for books to get more exposure and help to spread the message. Anxiety and related conditions should be discussed, not ignored. Only through being open and spreading the word, can we help people.

Thank you. Your support is very much appreciated.

Michelle Galler

77035580R00062

Made in the USA
Middletown, DE
17 June 2018